20/7/79.

ROCKS AND MAN

ROCKS AND MAN

Myra Shackley
Institute of Archaeology, University of Oxford

London
GEORGE ALLEN & UNWIN
Boston Sydney

First published in 1977

ISBN 0 04 913018 8

Printed in Great Britain
in 11/13 Baskerville
at the Alden Press, Oxford

For Mary

Preface

This book is designed to explore the ways in which human communities have exploited rocks, minerals and fossils as raw materials for their culture. Since it is intended to be of general interest, a strict archaeological or chronological framework has not been adopted, and examples are chosen unsystematically in place and time where they provide the clearest illustrations to the theme. Little basic knowledge is assumed and the introductory chapters, which deal with history and concepts, should convey enough background information to enable the rest of the book to be appreciated. It is possible to break down the archaeological record into a series of artefacts, life-systems and techniques, subdividing these into classes for studying the ways in which early peoples utilised the resources at their command. Unfortunately seldom is all the evidence of these activities preserved, and there is an additional source of error in the interpretation of available data. In some cases the literature of early civilisations is able to put some flesh on to dry archaeological bones, but historical sources do not really come into their own until Classical times. Wherever possible original historical material has been consulted, the texts being quoted where relevant. The writer makes no apology for omitting a consideration of metals, mining, and metal ores, since this forms a study in its own right.

General references and suggestions for further reading are grouped at the end of the book, together with a more detailed bibliography for each chapter.

M.L.S.
Woodstock

Acknowledgements

I am greatly indebted to Dr K. P. Oakley, Richard Bradley and Janet Davidson for their comments and criticisms, and for the provision of many helpful suggestions. Messrs M. Rouillard and N. J. Pollard have assisted with illustrations, and the following individuals have also contributed in various ways to the completion of this book: J. A. Ali, R. K. Annable, T. M. Ambrose, A. M. ApSimon, Professor B. W. Cunliffe, Professor G. Daniel, Mrs E. Hartley, Mrs S. E. C. Hawkes, J. Lavender, Dr D. P. S. Peacock, I. Sanders, Dr C. Singer.

Photographs and permissions have been kindly provided by The British Museum (Fig. 24), the British Museum (Department of Ethnography) (Figs 10, 11), The British Museum (Natural History) (Figs 29, 33), Devizes Museum (Figs 21, 23, 27), Institute of Geological Sciences (Figs 13, 15), London Express News and Features Service (Fig. 31), Miss Lynn Lewis and Bath Academy of Art (Fig. 21), Professor S. Piggott and Edinburgh University Press (Fig. 7), Suprintendza Antichita della Liguria (Fig. 22), Times Newspapers Ltd (Fig. 32), The Yorkshire Museum (Fig. 25).

Contents

List of Figures

Introduction

Throughout its formative stages the study of the antiquity of man has been inextricably connected with the development of geology. Indeed it was not until after the recognition of the processes of evolution and the significance of stratigraphy that the time-scale was lengthened to an extent which permitted the existence of any human pre-history at all. Now that these principles are universally accepted it seems salutary to remember that as late as the 17th century James Ussher, Archbishop of Armagh, was calculating that the evidence in the Old Testament indicated that the earth had been created in 4004 BC. Dr John Lightfoot, writing about the same time, refined this date to a precise '. . . man was created by the Trinity on October 23, 4004 BC at nine o'clock in the morning'.

In the ancient world savants had, of course, speculated about the origin and history of the earth and of man. Almost all cultures whose mythology has survived believed in some form of a 'Golden Age' when the connection between man and the gods was strongest, and they tended to hark back to this Utopian vision of perfection as something which could never be attained again. This often caused the early civilisations to have a somewhat inverted view of evolution, seeing man as becoming further and further away from perfection, instead of gradually approaching it. Odd references to geology occur in the works of the prehistoric civilizations, but in the main, one is dependent on the surviving literature of Greece and Rome, the former containing nearly all the scientific thought. Lucretius in *De Rerum Natura* describes his idea of human cultural evolution, '. . . the earliest weapons were hands, nails and teeth. Next came stones and branches wrenched from trees, and fire and flame as soon as they were discovered. Then man learnt to use tough iron and copper. Actually the use of copper was discovered before that of iron, because it is more easily handled and in more plentiful supply. By slow degrees the iron sword came to the fore, the bronze sickle came into disrepute; the ploughman began to cleave the earth with iron and on the darkling field of battle the odds were made even.' This is the prototype of the so-called 'three-age system' (stone–bronze–iron) which formed the basis of prehistoric chronology until very recent years, after it was refined and systematised by the Scandinavian archaeologists Thomsen and Worsaae. Although this passage suggests that Lucretius foresaw this development other parts of his work make it clear that he, in common with other learned men of his time, had no idea of the immense length of geological time. He refers to '. . . the multitudes of animals are formed out of the earth with the aid of showers and the sun's genial warmth'. Earlier scholars such as Aristotle had produced similar ideas, but there were few true men of science among the Greeks or Romans. The ethnographic observations of anthropologists or geographers such as Herodotus or Strabo are of some value, and the *Natural History* of Pliny the Elder is a fascinating collection of oddments combining the demonstrably impossible with the obviously true. Speculations on the origin of man are even found in a Chinese compilation dated to AD 52. Less attention was paid to the true study of geology, because it was more difficult to relate it directly to man, but there are occasional references to collectors of fossils, or to striking geological phenomena such as volcanism or earthquakes. The works of Theophrastus (*De Lapidibus*) and Vitruvius (*De Architectura*) are particularly useful when studying the Classical views of rocks and minerals.

After the sack of Alexandria in AD 640 there was a general decay in all forms of science amongst the European nations, and it is not until the Renaissance that empirical curiosity re-emerged. The first use of the word 'geology' in the accepted sense comes in the work of one Aldrovandus of Bologna, who died in 1606, although some of his work was based on that of Gorgius Agricola, who wrote his *De Natura Fossilia* in 1547. In the 17th and 18th centuries little attention was focused on events preceding the rise of the four greatest early empires (Assyria, Persia, Greece and Rome), and British antiquarians developed a deplorable tendency to fill the void between the known rise of these empires and the creation of the world by inventing mythical histories and peoples, in many ways an extension of the Classical idea envisaging the descent of man from the Gods. The formidable Dr Johnson, always critical of conjecture or speculation, stated firmly 'all that is known of the ancient state of Britain is a few pages, we can know no more than what old writers have told us'. The most widely held view of man's past was certainly the Biblical one, and until the late 19th century the Genesis account of the Creation, Fall and Flood was widely accepted, giving rise to calculations like those of Ussher.

A major development which presaged the rise of prehistoric archaeology was the recognition of the fact that human remains and artefacts could be found together in geologically ancient contexts. The first excavators had great difficulty in getting this fact accepted, and received formidable opposition from reputable scholars. The earliest significant realisation of the causal association between stone tools and man was made by John Frere (1740–1807), who had been investigating the deposits of the gravel pit at Hoxne, Suffolk, later to be recognised as one of the most important Palaeolithic (Stone Age) sites in Britain. Little notice was taken at the time of his find, but it is significant in that he recorded in print the association between artefacts, extinct animals and undisturbed geological strata. The next important link in the chain of events was forged in France by the work of an amateur geologist, Boucher de Perthes, who collected flint implements from the Somme gravels, especially in the area of Abbeville. Between 1838, a year which marked the first exhibition of his finds, and 1847 he reached the conclusion that the types of association noted by Frere could not be fitted into any diluvian theory (after the Flood), and he then produced his famous three-volume text *Antiquités Celtiques et Antédiluviennes* and later *De l'homme antédiluvien et ses oevres* (Paris, 1860). In England the major authorities to be converted to these new views were undoubtedly Sir John Prestwich (1812–1896) and Sir John Evans (1823–1908). The latter visited Perthes at Abbeville, and agreed with his conclusions that the axes which the latter had found were undoubtedly in association with undisturbed beds of gravel, meaning that their makers must have lived at the same time as the deposition of the gravel, 'when the deluge, or whatever was the origin of these gravels, took place'.

After this watershed in the 1860s geology and archaeology went forward apace. By the late 1860s pre-history was a reputable study, and in 1865 Sir John Lubbock's *Prehistoric Times* became a best-seller. The refinement of the three-age system and the appreciation of a series of new prehistoric sites followed shortly afterwards, and from this period when the antiquity of man became fully realised, it became the task of the geologists to provide a backcloth for that antiquity, based on the newly discovered principle of stratigraphy. This fact, established by Sir Charles Lyell, stated that, unless disturbed, the oldest layers of rock were to be found at the base of a series and the youngest at the top, or that 'unless you stir them up the discarded letters in your waste-paper basket will have earlier dates near the bottom and later dates at the top' (Stuart Piggott). Archaeologists realised soon after that the layers on archaeological sites could be studied in the same way, and that for each site a coherent sequence of occupation could be worked out in terms of the successive strata.

The task of reconstructing the complete history of man is far from over, and with every passing year pre-history is being pushed further and further back in time. The relationship between man and his environment becomes progressively closer with increasing antiquity, until a point is reached where man is exerting hardly any influence at all over his surroundings; yet the converse of this statement is of paramount importance. In the remote past man, or proto-man (hominids) becomes himself just a part of the geological record, no more important than any other species. As time goes on the man/environment relationship gradually changes and the links become less well defined, since man is able to modify his surroundings with varying degrees of precision and success. In addition, when we enter historical time, the sources of information about human activity are multiplied, and we are no longer forced to rely solely on artefact or faunal associations for ideas of culture and environment.

It follows, therefore, that the connections between man and rocks are twofold, depending on the age of the human culture being studied. Thus we can consider both man *in* rocks and man *with* rocks, using the term rock to include subsidiary mineral and fossil inclusions. Man progresses from being a fossil to studying his own fossilised ancestors. In talking about the relationship between rocks and man in prehistoric time we are talking principally about the exploitation of mineral, fossil and stone resources, and the ways in which this exploitation is documented in the archaeological record.

Throughout the entire history of man his relationship with his environment has remained crucial, and is nowhere better reflected than in a study of the stages and variations in resource exploitation. The rocks which compose this planet have been crucial for the development of man as a species; indeed, since they furnished the material for early tools, they were practically responsible for it. Even today man is dependent in many ways on rocks, not least as a source of 'fossil' fuels and as raw material for the technology of civilisation. The rocks of this earth are not only our most significant resource but also the only one which is completely irreplaceable. The following chapters try to examine the ways in which man has used this resource, and how this use has been reflected in the evidence of material culture.

CHAPTER 1

Earth history

'...τί τῶν κοινῶν κάτω
καὶ εὐγγενικῶν δύναιτ' ἂν ἄνθρωπον φυγεῖν'

Alexis, 372–300 BC

(. . . *if men have probed*
Worlds far remote, can problems of this earth,
This common home to which we're born, defy them?)

Geology (Greek *ge*, the earth, *logos*, discourse) is the scientific discipline concerned with the history of the earth, the study of the material of which it is composed and the processes and events which produced its appearance. The scope of the subject is vast, both in time and space, encompassing everything from explaining the present configuration of the continents to tracing the evolution of a particular species of plant or animal. Such a vast field is of necessity divided into a number of more specialised branches, including palaeontology (the study of the plants and animals which lived on the earth in the past, and which are now preserved as fossils) and stratigraphy (the methods used for distinguishing the different layers, or strata, of rock from a study of their fossil and mineral components). Historical geology considers the history of the earth as recorded in the sequences of rocks, and structural geology examines the ways in which these rock units are disposed and the processes which have formed them. Mineralogy, petrology and geochemistry are concerned with various aspects of the composition of the rocks. The last major branch of the subject, physical geology, includes sub-disciplines which could be also included with geography, namely geomorphology (the classification and description of landscapes and the ways in which they were formed) and pedology (the study of soils).

The very earliest history of the earth as a planet is still a controversial subject, and one which remains intimately connected with astronomy. It has, however, been established that the earth shares a common origin with the other planets of the solar system, all of which were formed from the parent material of our sun by some catastrophic event in the extremely remote past. At the earliest stage the earth was a spinning globe of uniformly hot, molten material, at first cooling rather rapidly, principally by heat radiating into space. The heavier, less easily oxidised elements such as iron and nickel became concentrated near the centre to produce the core (or 'nife') of the earth (Fig. 1), which lies from a depth of 1800 miles (2900 km) to the centre. It has a temperature of 2700°C and various unique properties, partly those of a liquid. Outside this core lies the mantle, at a depth of 22–1800 miles (35–2900 km), which consists mainly of heavy silicate minerals such as olivine, rich in magnesium. The outermost crust of the earth is divided into two layers, the lower (inner) one, some 9–12 miles (15–20 km) thick, being given the name 'sima' (from its two principal components, silica and magnesium) and the upper

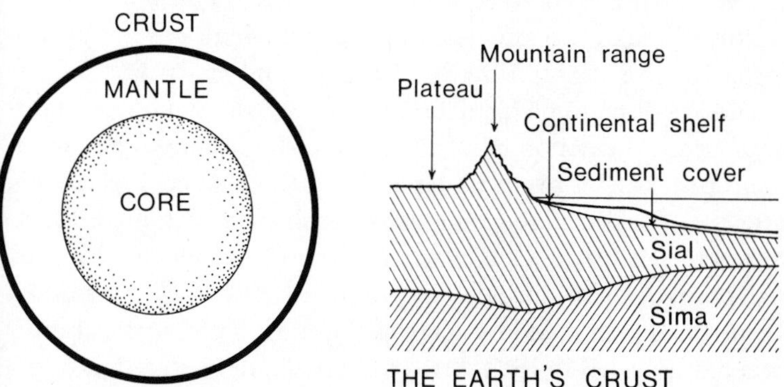

Figure 1. Diagrammatic structure of the earth, showing the relationship between the *sial* and *sima* layers.

one, 6–12 miles (10–20 km) thick, called 'sial' (silica and aluminium), discontinuous and forming the continental masses. Over this upper crust lies a thin skin of sedimentary deposits and above this a very fine layer of soil and recently deposited alluvium. The crust, which is thickest under mountain ranges and plateaux, is made of crystalline rocks, which are sometimes exposed on the surface where they have been affected by the great mountain-building periods, or covered by later sediments. Such areas are called 'shields', examples being found in Canada and in the Baltic, which have been subject to continuous cyclic processes of weathering, erosion and deposition and modification since the beginning of geological time. The result of these processes is a sequence of superimposed layers of different rocks, conventionally divided into three principal types: igneous, crystalline or glassy rocks formed through the consolidation of molten material; sedimentary, material derived from pre-existing rocks; and metamorphic, rocks changed by heat or pressure.

This complex cycle of geological processes is responsible for the appearance of the rocks as they can be seen today, and may have been repeated many times during the production of a single rock. The earth is constantly being modified by the breakdown of existing rocks and the formation and modification of new ones. Today a new factor has entered the cycle, that of man himself, who alters the appearance of the planet by mining and quarrying, and large scale modifications of the landscape. Natural breakdown processes include weathering, such phenomena as frost shattering by freezing and expansion of the included water, biological breakdown by the action of plants or animals, the action of rainwater and the selective disintegration of rocks as a result of exposure to the elements. Erosional processes consist of the removal of such degradation products by a series of agents such as wind, water or glaciers, which then redeposited them in new locations so that they eventually formed new rocks. At any stage in the erosional cycle fossils may become included in the fabric of the rock, and be used as a tool for distinguishing the different strata.

The second major group of earth processes includes those

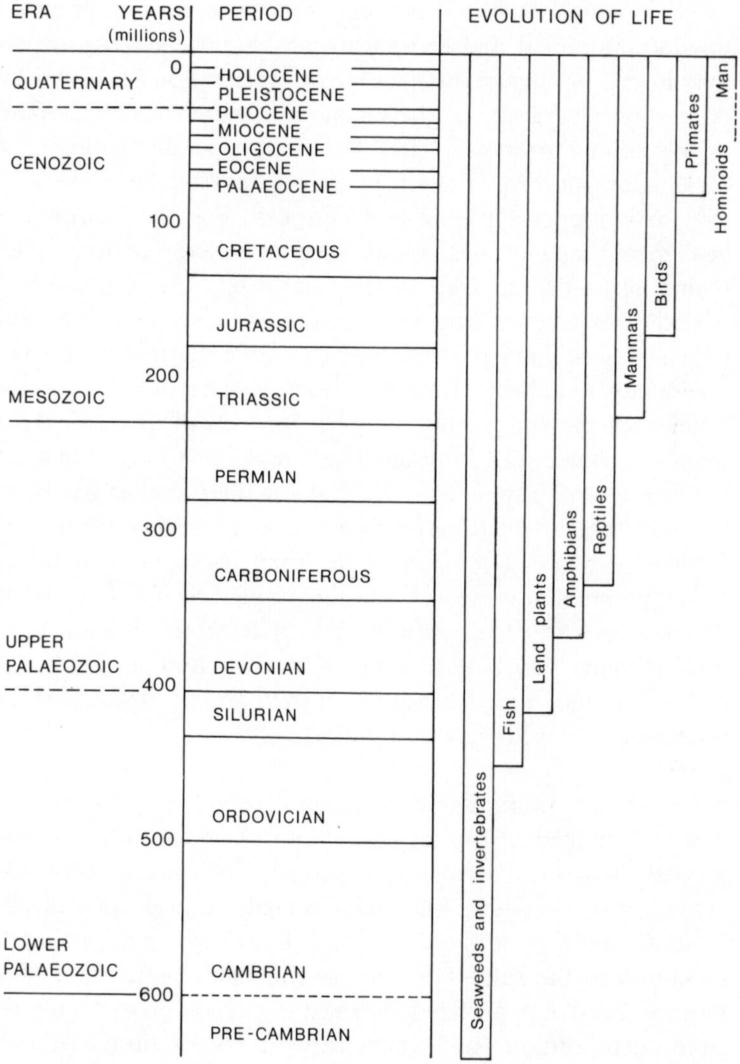

ERA	YEARS (millions)	PERIOD
QUATERNARY	0	HOLOCENE
		PLEISTOCENE
CENOZOIC		PLIOCENE
		MIOCENE
		OLIGOCENE
		EOCENE
		PALAEOCENE
	100	CRETACEOUS
		JURASSIC
MESOZOIC	200	TRIASSIC
		PERMIAN
	300	CARBONIFEROUS
UPPER PALAEOZOIC		DEVONIAN
	400	SILURIAN
		ORDOVICIAN
	500	
LOWER PALAEOZOIC		CAMBRIAN
	600	PRE-CAMBRIAN

EVOLUTION OF LIFE: Seaweeds and invertebrates; Fish; Land plants; Amphibians; Reptiles; Mammals; Birds; Primates; Hominoids; Man

Figure 2. The stratigraphic time scale showing major conventional divisions and a broad outline of the evolution of life-forms.

which take place within or through the crust of the earth, as a result of physical or chemical activity within the crust or mantle, as opposed to weathering or erosion which occur above the surface. Examples of such processes are earthquakes and volcanic activity. All are still going on in a continuing cycle, now accompanied and complicated by human activity which may hasten or change them, as in the acceleration of erosion by vegetation clearance, or the changes in patterns of river flow as a result of irrigation. The formation and modification of rocks is an inexorable chain of events, making the history of the earth immensely long and complex. For this reason the geological time scale has been divided into a series of time-units, including four great eras divided into a number of geological periods, each containing the deposits of a geological system which may be named after the area where the rocks are most commonly found or where they were first recognized, or on account of the composition or fossil contents of the rock. This sequence is arranged in order from the oldest to the youngest, making a stratigraphic column (Fig. 2), the divisions based on the evidence provided by fossils, with the exception of the pre-Cambrian rocks. The crust of the earth is thought to be at least 4500 million years old, and the simplest forms of life (such as bacteria and algae) can be traced back to at least 3500 million years ago. Strata more than 600 million years old seldom contain any fossils, and it is therefore impossible to use them for world-wide correlations.

Minerals are the fundamental units of which rocks are composed, homogeneous solids of definite chemical composition, formed by natural inorganic processes. Such a definition includes ice as a mineral but excludes coal, natural gas and oil. Natural mercury (quicksilver) is a liquid mineral, the only exception to the rule. The definite chemical composition of a mineral need not be fixed or constant, since many minerals have a composition which varies between certain limits without altering their fundamental properties, the atomic structure remaining constant through the mineral units. The term 'mineral' often has a more extended usage, and may be used to describe anything of economic value which can be extracted from the earth, even clay or coal. A rock, on the other hand, has no fixed chemical composition, is not homogeneous and has no definite shape of its own. In most cases it will consist of mixtures of several minerals. Granite, for example, is composed of the minerals feldspar, quartz and mica, but some rocks may be formed mainly from one mineral. Ancient Classical mineralogy consisted simply of descriptions of various ores, precious and semi-precious stones, but today the identification of minerals and their properties is a science in its own right. As the names of minerals indicate, much of the Greek information was clearly derived from the East, and Roman 'scientific' literature contains little new information. Minerals are identified today by their physical and chemical properties (colour, lustre, transparency, taste and odour), by other characteristics depending on their shape and form (cleavage planes, hardness and fracture), by crystallography and by their optical properties. The colour may often be the most striking feature, but it is not an infallible guide to identification since it may vary between two specimens of the same mineral. Quartz (silicon dioxide) for example, is generally white or colourless, but may be green, brown, pinkish-yellow or black. The colour of a mineral depends on the nature and arrangement of the constituent ions, thus minerals chiefly composed of aluminium, potassium, calcium, magnesium, or barium are frequently colourless, while those with much chromium, iron, manganese, cobalt, titanium, vanadium or copper are coloured. There was a strong tendency for early mineralogy to be based solely on colour, which lends some measure of doubt to the exact stone being referred to in some descriptions. The practice is still, however, common in the present day, and many existing antiquities made of mineral substances have been wrongly described in the past by archaeologists with no geological knowledge. The lustre of a mineral depends on the character of the light reflected by it. Vitreous lustre, the lustre of broken glass, is shown by quartz and rock salt, amber and opal show resinous lustre, gypsum is silky and diamond adamantine. In some cases the feel, taste and smell of the mineral may also be diagnostic, for example the sulphurous smell given off by pyrites when struck, or the saline flavour of rock salt. Another property less commonly used in identification is the streak of the mineral, or its colour in a finely divided state determined by scratching it across a piece of unglazed porcelain. This was mentioned by Aristotle who says that 'Some kinds of stones give rise to different colours when rubbed like . . ., which are black, but which make white marks' (*De Coloribus*, III, 793a). The hardness and fracture of the mineral may also be helpful in identification. A good example of this is seen in the conchoidal (shell-like) fracture (p. 48) of flint. Magnetic properties were recognised very early in time, and Plato says that the word 'magnetis' was first applied to loadstone (magnetite, Fe_3O_4) by Euripides (Ion 533). Lucretius also records that 'iron rings jump up and filings rave in brass bowls when the magnet stone is placed underneath' (*De Rerum Natura* VI, 1046), and the electrostatic properties of jet and amber probably contributed to their popularity as gemstones.

Under favourable conditions minerals are found as crystals, which helps in their identification, but the form of the substance is not always dependent on crystals, as is frequently supposed. A crystal may be defined as 'a body bounded by surfaces, usually flat, arranged on a definite plan which is an extension of the internal arrangement of the atoms'. The shape, or morphology of a crystal is diagnostic in many cases. A method of describing crystal systems has been devised, based on the number, length and inclination of each axis. Six main divisions are recognised (cubic, tetragonal, hexagonal, orthorhombic, monoclinic and triclinic) each with subdivisions named after one of the minerals which belongs to them. Thus in the cubic system, where the crystals have three equal axes set at right angles to one another, there are three subdivisions, the galena type, the pyrite type and the tetrahedrite. In an examination of a rock the mineral components are usually studied in thin sections or as small grains, and are identified under the microscope on the basis of their optical properties. This is a complex procedure which takes a long time to learn, but it has formed the basis of a great deal of work in archaeological science on the identification of rock types and their sources (p. 50). Thin slices of rock are cut, cemented to a microscope slide and ground down to a uniform thickness of 30 μm, then examined under ordinary and polarised light uiing a petrological microscope. The minerals are distinguished by their crystal form, cleavage, transparency, colour and refractive index, and, under polarised light or crossed nichols, by their pleochroism, extinction angles, polarisation colours and the occurrence of special forms such as twinning. Rocks and ceramics may also be identified by 'heavy mineral' analysis, a heavy mineral being one with a specific gravity greater than 2.9.

The term 'rock' may be applied to any mass of minerals, whether or not they are consolidated. Thus a loose mass of gravel is still, by definition, a rock. The main rock-forming minerals are the silicates, carbonates and oxides, with lesser quantities of sulphates, chlorides and phosphates and accessory minerals which are not as significant when the mineral composition is being assessed for rock classification. Sedimentary rocks are derived by erosion and weathering from pre-existing rocks, and are laid down in strata differentiated on the basis of their composition, grain size or colour. The zone of separation between these layers is referred to as a bedding plane, and the whole series is termed stratified. Sedimentary rocks may be detrital (composed of agglomerations of particles of minerals from previous rocks) with pebbly, sandy or clayey texture, chemical or organic in origin, such as diatomite (formed by the accumulation of the siliceous remains of some microscopic plants). Organic rocks also include those formed from macroscopic plant materials, such as peat, lignite and coal. Travertine, or flowstone, is an example of a chemically formed rock, accumulating in caves as a result of water containing dissolved carbonates acting on calcareous rocks. Stalagmites and stalactites are formed as a result of the same process. Sedimentary rocks are also divided up on the basis of their cementing material, which may be siliceous, calcareous, dolomitic, ferruginous or argillaceous. Siliceous sandstones are very durable but calcareous and dolomitic sandstones (cemented with calcium carbonate) rather less so. Limestone, which primarily consists of calcium carbonate, may either be formed by precipitation from sea water or as small spheroidal (oolitic) grains, or it may be the result of the accumulation of the shells and skeletons of marine organisms which are then cemented together by calcium carbonate in solution. Limestones often contain fragments of fossils, which may give them an especially attractive appearance, such as the famous 'crinoidal marble' (p. 36), technically a hard crinoidal limestone. The mace head shown in Figure 3 was found in association with a primary inhumation burial of the Wessex culture, at Bush Barrow in Wiltshire. It is made of a rare type of limestone consisting mainly of the Devonian stromatoporid coral (p. 36) *Amphipora ramosa*. It was thought to have originally had a wooden handle with a brass ornament on the top, the latter being fastened to the top of the handle by a brass pin. These features have been reproduced in the facsimile of the handle, the originals being much decayed. The mace head came from an especially rich grave which produced several gold items, bronze daggers and axes and a hammered gold belt-hook with incised ornament. It is thought that the rock for the mace head probably came from the New Red Sandstone of Teignmouth in Devon. The burial was one of the

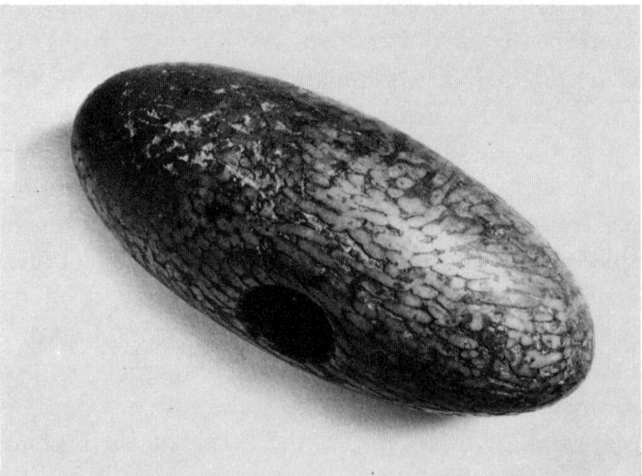

Figure 3. Mace-head from a 'Wessex' culture burial at Bush Barrow, Wiltshire. It is made of a rare type of limestone containing the Devonian stromatoporid coral *Amphipora ramosa*, which probably came from pebbles in the New Red Sandstone of Teignmouth, Devon. (Photo, Nick Pollard)

so-called 'royal' graves of the Early Bronze Age 'Wessex' culture, dating to the 2nd millennium BC. The objects were associated with the extended skeleton of a man, orientated north–south under a barrow, who had been buried with a large lozenge-shaped gold plate on his breast, and with these other very rich grave goods. It seems probable that the types of particularly attractive stone used for axes and mace heads were chosen not only for their appearance but also for their rarity value and more tenuous features such as supposed magical powers. This particular stone, which is calcareous and rather soft, is not at all suitable for a weapon, and was presumably employed because of its attractive markings. A similar occurrence is the Jurassic serpulid limestone which probably occurred as an erratic block and was used for two fine polished Neolithic axes (Fig. 4) found at Bury St Edmonds (Suffolk), which was a far less suitable material for an axe than the local harder rocks and was obviously chosen for some less practical reason.

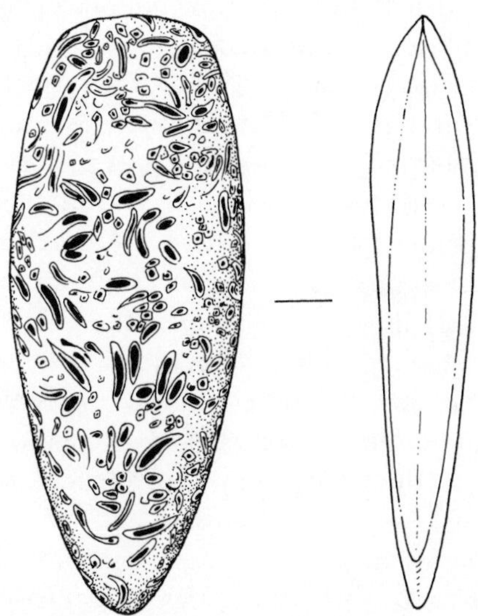

Figure 4. Polished Neolithic axe from Bury St Edmunds, Suffolk, made from Jurassic *serpulid* limestone probably obtained locally as an erratic block. (J. Evans Collection, Ashmolean Museum, Oxford)

Sedimentary rocks have the advantage of well-defined stratification planes (bedding planes) along which they can be split, making it easier to obtain suitable building stones (p. 79). In Britain stone was not systematically quarried for building until Roman times, although it was roughly worked millennia earlier. Some of the earliest British examples of stone masonry show a high degree of technological expertise achieved with rudimentary tools, for example the construction of megalithic tombs in the Neolithic or the mortice and tenon joints which attached the great lintels to the uprights in the trilithon circle of Stonehenge. The majority of the stones of Stonehenge, including the trilithons, are sarsen-stone (an Eocene sandstone with siliceous cement, sometimes called 'quartzite sandstone').

Igneous rocks are the product of volcanic activity, where molten rock material (magma) has solidified. 'Intrusive' igneous rocks invade the surrounding strata without ever reaching the surface, while 'extrusive' igneous rocks (such as lava flows) are pushed or blown out above ground. The igneous rocks are divided into three groups, plutonic, hypabyssal and volcanic. The plutonic group, occurring as intrusive material solidified under slow cooling well below the surface of the earth, are crystalline and coarse grained, such as granite, syenite, diorite and gabbro. The hypabyssal group, such as the porphyries, occur as inclusions which have solidified into dykes and sills well below the surface, and are much finer grained although still crystalline. Volcanic rocks are formed as quickly cooled surface extrusions, and include the volcanic glasses as well as fine-grained crystalline rocks such as ryolite, andesite or basalt. Obsidian and the other volcanic glasses were much prized as raw materials for stone tool manufacture, due to their attractive shine, durability and sharp conchoidal fracture. Fragmentary rocks such as tuffs, ashes and volcanic agglomerates are often associated with volcanic igneous rocks. Pumice, also an igneous rock, is a light cellular lava chiefly composed of aluminium silicate. It had many different uses in the ancient world, both as a depilatory and as an abrasive. Catullus comments on the use of pumice for smoothing the ends (*frontes*) of rolls of parchment, and it is often spoken of by other poets as part of the general equipment of a scribe, along with ruler, pencils, pens, ink pots and penknife. Propertius compares the fine polish of his verses to the smooth look of a pumice-polished page, '*Exactus tenui pumice uersus eat*' (Propertius, Elegies III.i.8). When considered as building stones igneous rocks have the disadvantage of being harder to work than metamorphic or sedimentary rocks, but will often take a high polish. They were therefore used chiefly for monumental masonry, floor slabs or pavings, and wall linings. As far back as early Dynastic times in Egypt roughly dressed granite was used for these purposes, but generally little architectural use was made of such rocks before Classical times.

Metamorphic rocks result from changes in pre-existing rocks due to pressure and temperature. The resulting composition of the rock depends, obviously, on the composition of the original, and on the type and intensity of the metamorphism. Quartzite, one of the commonest metamorphic rocks, is a result of the alteration of sandstone, and one of the commonest forms of marble is a metamorphosed limestone.

Some rocks may be almost entirely composed of fossils, like the stromatoporid limestone already mentioned and the distinctive nummulitic limestone, one variety of which was used for the greater part of the Giza pyramids. This was an Eocene rock made from billions of round foraminifera of the species *Nummulites gizehensis* and was remarked on by the geographer Strabo who made a rather charming mis-identification 'Among the heaps of stone chips lying at the foot of the Pyramids some are found that are like lentils in form and size . . . they say that what was left of the food of the workmen has petrified, and this is not improbable'. (Strabo, *Geography* XVII, 1.)

Such fossils are the visible remains of prehistoric life, or the negative evidence that some form of life once existed. In order to have become fossilised a plant or animal must have had some hard parts (bone, perhaps, or shell), have been very quickly buried and remained undisturbed throughout the long processes of fossilisation. Because of these conditions only a very small proportion of the plants and animals which die are preserved as fossils. In very rare cases a whole animal may be preserved, such as the 'deep frozen' mammoths from Siberia, or the intact Iron Age bodies recovered from peat bogs in Denmark which are very recent fossils indeed. There are, however, only a few sets of burial conditions which will permit perfect preservation of this kind, including extreme cold and acid groundwater which inhibits the action of aerobic bacteria which cause decay. Extreme dryness may also preserve tissue, a fact exploited in predynastic Egypt where burials made without coffins in the hot, dry, sand were remarkably well preserved, a discovery leading eventually to mummification, an artificial way to obtain the same result by using desiccating agents and preservatives. It is notably less efficient than the natural process. The soft parts of animals are very rarely preserved as fossils, with the exception of the cases already mentioned and finds of insects which have been trapped in amber resin. Leaves and small animals may sometimes be preserved if they have been trapped in mud which then hardened into shale, leaving behind as a film of carbon both their general form and quite fine details of structure.

The hard parts of animals are more common as fossils, although even these are rarely complete. Whole logs and trunks of trees may occur intact in peat bogs, both in those of Recent origin and those from the Coal Measures of the Carboniferous. It is, however, rare that the hard parts of animals are recovered in their original state. Water will dissolve the chemicals which form the shells or bones, leaving them light and spongy, and sometimes these chemicals are replaced by others, especially silica, lime, or iron compounds. A well-known example of this occurs in the Chalk, where the shells of sea-urchins (echinoids) have often become filled with flint, deposited inside the hollow mould of the fossil from percolating siliceous ground water. The Jurassic shales of the Lyme Regis area of Devon are particularly famous for their ammonites (p. 145) preserved in iron pyrites, an attractive shiny yellow mineral sometimes called 'Fool's Gold', which has made these fossils prized by collectors. The mineral replacement may preserve the structure of the individual perfectly, or it may show only the general form. Another class of fossils, already mentioned, are the moulds or casts, where the original material composing the plant or animal has been dissolved away so that only a hollow cast remains, the walls of which are a natural mould of the fossil. This may later be filled in with other substances, as in the case of echinoids, or may just be left as a void. Other, less spectacular, types of fossil include the borings of worms and molluscs into stone, such as the marine pebbles bored by the mollusc *Pholas* which are now found in shingle beaches raised many hundreds of feet above present sea level. Coprolite (fossil faeces) is yet another type of fossil. The rarest fossils are, of course, those of man himself and his ancestors. Fossils are generally, but not always, recovered from sedimentary rocks, the rare exceptions to this rule including the fossil hominid bones and teeth recovered from volcanic tuffs at Olduvai Gorge, Tanzania.

The evidence provided by fossils is of the greatest importance in the reconstruction of geological history. Each system of stratified rocks is characterised by particular combinations of animal and plant genera, and each smaller division (series and stages) by the recognition of species which may not occur in the divisions immediately above or below it, or which may occur in markedly different proportions. The changes in the fossil record may be very gradual, one species being found in greater numbers at the top of a rock zone than it is at the bottom, and this enables rocks of the same character to be subdivided into 'belts' and 'zones' on the basis of their fossil inclusions. Sometimes changes may be very drastic, a species totally disappearing in a relatively short period of geological time. This type of evidence permits rocks in different areas to be correlated, always bearing in mind that the genera and species found will never be entirely identical, due to climatic and other related fluctuations. Conclusions can also be drawn from the the fossil evidence concerning the conditions under which the rock formation was deposited. It is comparatively easy to distinguish a marine from a land species, and it is often possible to make deductions concerning such factors as the depth and temperature of the ancient sea, the proximity of the shoreline or the nature of the palaeoclimate, principally by drawing analogies with the habitat of species living today.

Fossils are also of primary importance to the biologist for tracing the paths of evolution, and for studying the remains of groups of organisms which have now become extinct, but the life record is unfortunately incomplete because of breaks in the succession of stratified rocks due to denudation and other earth processes.

By far the greatest number of fossil species which turn up in archaeological contexts are invertebrates (animals without backbones), most of which once lived in the sea and many of which are now extinct. Invertebrates are divided into ten major groups, and Figure 5 illustrates some of their structures. The lowest and simplest forms of animals are the Protozoa, such as *Amoeba* or *Globigerina*, which are very small in size, often consisting of only one cell. Clearly individual fossils can never be found. The structure of sponges (Porifera) is more complicated since they are multicellular animals. Water is drawn into the sack-like body through the pores, and swept along by the flagella of the collar cells. Microscopic food particles are then extracted from the water, which is eventually expelled through the top opening. The skeleton of the sponge may be made from flexible spongin fibres, or from needle-like mineral spicules of silica or lime. Perfect sponges are rare as fossils but the spicules are quite common, and casts of them in iron pyrites are known from the Menevian Beds of St Davids. Fossil sponge remains in the Chalk are particularly abundant, and the silica from sponge spicules contributed largely to the formation of flint. Individual members of the Coelenterata are better represented in the fossil record, a group which includes sea-anemones, jelly-fish and corals, all of which are aquatic and radially symmetrical. These have only one internal cavity (the coelenteron) from which the group gets its name, which opens onto the interior of the animal via the mouth. The graptolites, a group of organisms found only in Lower Palaeozoic rocks, especially shales, are rare even in sandstones and limestones. They were rather small, but compound, and the

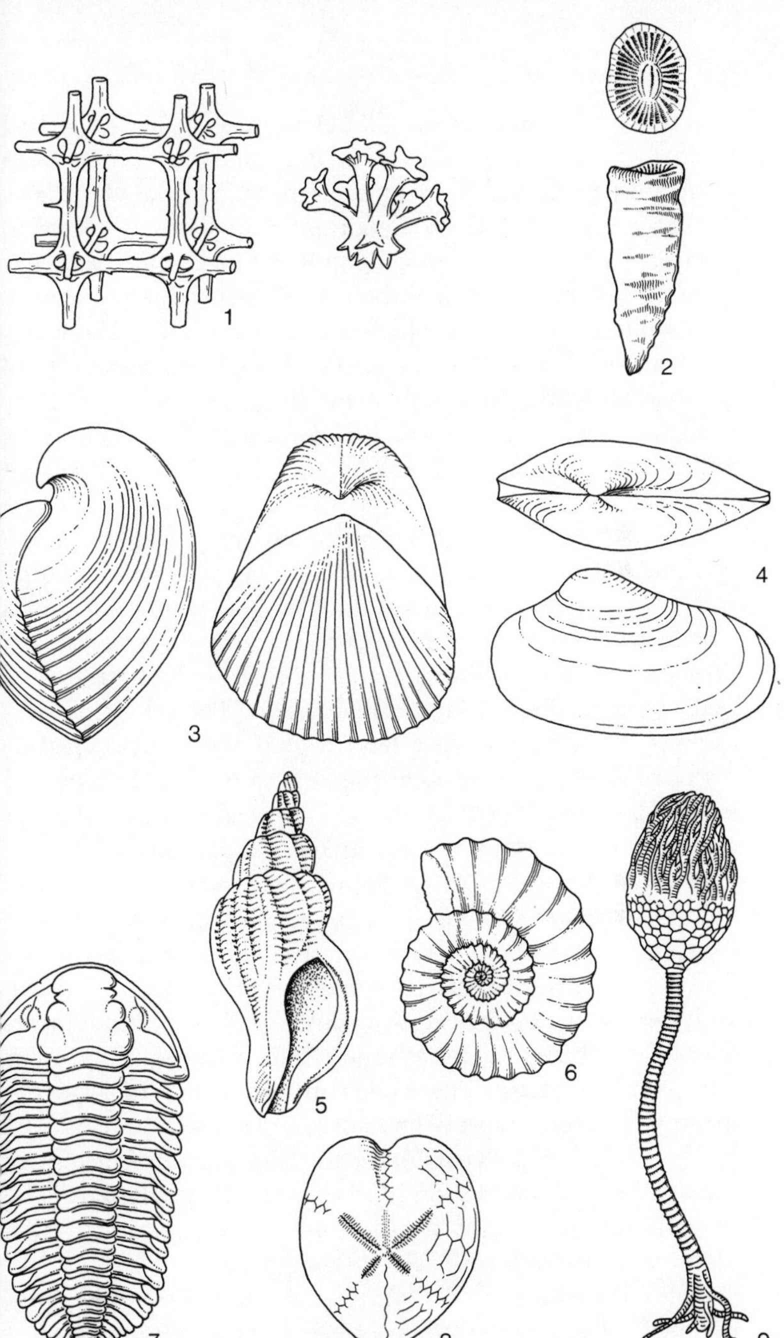

Figure 5. Structure of some of the main groups of invertebrate fossils: (1) a sponge and sponge spicules, (2) fossil coral, (3) a brachiopod, (4) a lamellibranch, (5) a gastropod, (6) an ammonite, (7) a trilobite, (8) an echinoid, and (9) a crinoid.

structure of their soft parts is still unknown. They lived attached to floating seaweed or were free floating, and they seem to have been able to survive even at some distance from the shore. *Millipora* coral is still an important rock-forming organism today as reef coral building islands, although they are confined nowadays to an equatorial belt of warm sheltered waters, with a minimum water temperature of 70°F (21°C). The water needs to be clear and shallow, the corals being incapable of growing at depths greater than 150 ft (45 m) because of their need for light. Fossil reef corals are, however, much more widely distributed, and many are important petroleum reservoirs.

Echinoids (which together with crinoids are part of the phylum Echinodermata) are also marine animals, including star-fishes, sea-urchins and sea lilies, as well as other members which are now extinct. Nearly all have a hard calcareous skeleton, usually forming a complete shell or 'test', and they make some of the most spectacular fossils. The echinoids (sea-urchins) themselves usually have a globular, heart-shaped or discoidal body, covered with spines. Figure 5 shows a typical echinoid, which lived in the sea especially where the sea bed was rocky, sandy or calcareous. Many species have a very long time range and are found as far back as the Cretaceous. The crinoids (sea-lilies) were animals which looked more like plants, and whose bodies consisted of a stem and a calyx which contained the digestive and other important organs, with long movable arms growing out of it. The stem fragments of crinoids are much more common fossils than any of the other parts, and are sometimes sufficiently numerous to form the major part of some types of limestone, for example the 'crinoidal marble', which has been subject to some degree of metamorphosis since its formation during the Carboniferous. The crinoids appear to have lived in shallow water, and are often found in association with reef building corals.

In the Brachiopoda (Fig. 5), the soft parts of the animal are enclosed in a shell, which is formed in two parts (valves) of unequal size. Nearly all extant brachiopods are small marine invertebrates which live fixed to a rock or some other object, but it seems that some earlier forms were free floating. Brachiopods may grow to enormous sizes, up to 12 in. (30 cm) across, and the shape of the shell is very varied. All were marine and seem to have preferred shallow water where the bottom was rocky or stony. Two hundred species are known at present but at least 30 000 fossil forms once existed, dating back as far as the Cambrian. The shells are extremely common fossils and seem often to have been selected by early man for use in the manufacture of jewellery.

The Mollusca on the other hand, include both land, freshwater and marine species, and also form some of the most common fossils. Lamellibranchs have a calcareous shell made from two valves, like brachiopods, but instead of lying above and below the body of the animal they are on the right and left side, joined by means of a hinge and a ligament. The foot, which protrudes from the ventral surface, enabled the animal to crawl or to burrow in sand or mud. The shell can be closed by means of muscles and the two halves may often be ornamented with ribs, tubercules or spines. A few genera moved by the rapid closing of the valves, causing water to be expelled and propelling the animal forward, and others, such as the oyster were permanently attached to the rock. The species *Spondylus* is one of the commonest occurring in archaeological contexts, having an irregularly shaped shell with the right valve larger than the left. It lived originally in warm seas and was found as far back as the Jurassic. *Spondylus gaederopus* was extensively imported into Central Europe from the Mediterranean, and used for the manufacture of jewellery in early Neolithic times (4th millennium BC). Its distribution has been used as evidence for the rapid spread of the Neolithic way of life in Europe from the earliest sites in the Balkans. *Pecten* has an oval or sub-circular shell, and is very widespread in rocks from the Carboniferous to the present day. Other popular forms include *Cardium* (the cockle) with a convex or cordate shell. Its serrated edge was used to decorate the Mediterranean impressed pottery (cardial technique) of the early Neolithic farmers, dating to 5000–3500 BC. The pottery is simple in shape but profusely decorated with shell imprints (Fig. 6). The shell

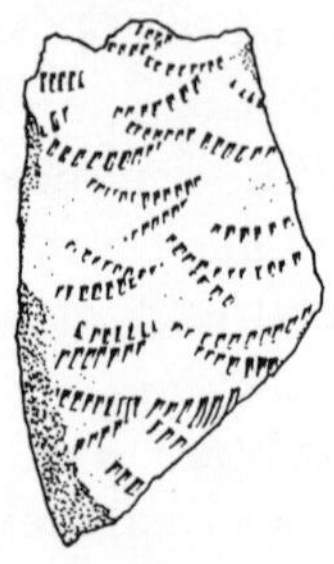

Figure 6. Early Neolithic potsherd, decorated by impressions made with *Cardium* shells.

crops up again later in time as a medieval pilgrim badge, a sign that its wearer had made the pilgrimage to the shrine of St James at Compostella in Spain. Another class of mollusca, the Gastropods, includes the snail, whelk and cowrie. The shell is made of a single piece and may be of almost any shape, but in most cases it consists of a long tube open at one end and tapering to a point at the other. The tube is coiled into a spiral, each coil being termed a whorl. As the animal crawls along the shell is carried on the dorsal surface of its body. Some gastropods live on land, but by far the greatest numbers are marine. The commonest species which occur in archaeological contexts are *Patella* (with a conical shell), *Strombus*, *Sypho* and *Murex* which is the source of the famous Tyrian purple dye. In Palaeozoic and Mesozoic rocks the gastropods are generally less abundant than the Lamellibranchs, although they exceed them today. Miocene gastropod shells have been found in the deposits of the Neolithic temples of Malta, together with carved limestone helicoids modelled on details of their internal casts. The straight, narrow cone-shaped gastropods known as *Dentalium* resemble canine teeth, and as such seem to have been kept by early man (p. 108).

The most spectacular fossil molluscs often culturally associated with man are the Ammonites (Fig. 5). Although extinct since the end of the Cretaceous period they were closely related to the pearly nautilus of modern seas. Ammonites and nautiloids are members of the class of molluscs named Cephalopoda, which includes octopus, squids and cuttle-fish. Like the shell of the nautilus ammonites were coiled into a planulate spiral which inevitably led to a comparison with snakes. Several species of ammonite are shown in Figure 34 (p. 146), including *Hildoceras*, which has a flattened shell with a prominent 'keel' on the edge. The ribs on the shell are typically sickle-shaped and the whorls low and subquadrate in section. The species comes from the upper Lias. *Dactylioceras* is found in the same formation, but its ribs are more sinuous and of a different shape, straight at first and then bifurcate. The ammonites as a group have a fairly short geological range, becoming extinct after the deposition of the Chalk. All were marine and free swimming, facilitated by the buoyancy of the air chambers in the shell, but they seem to have lived at no great distance from the land. Fossil ammonites were occasionally perforated and used by prehistoric man, for example the three specimens of *Aspidoceras lissoceratoides* from a Solutrean III layer at Fourneau du Diable (Bourdeilles, France) which are now in Les Eyzies museum. Mesolithic rock paintings in south-eastern Spain show similar forms, and the drawing of a spiral is an essential feature of the secret ritual of the old men in some Australian Aboriginal tribes.

One of the last orders of molluscs, the Dibranchiata, includes the living cuttle-fish and the extinct belemnites, of which the internal guard is the most common fossil evidence. It is generally cigar-shaped but varies in length, the rest of the skeleton being seldom found. Belemnites seem to have been free swimming animals, equipped with ten arms ending in suckers and an ink sac like the squid. The function of the guard was probably to counteract the buoyancy of the rest of the body, and to maintain a horizontal position for swimming.

The last group of invertebrate animals to be considered is the huge phylum of Arthropoda, which includes the crustaceans, insects and spiders. Most members of it breathe by means of gills (as in crabs and lobsters) and have a hard, chitinous exoskeleton. Trilobites existed only during Palaeozoic times, forming one of the most striking features of the fauna of that period. Their bodies were three lobed (hence the name) and divided by furrows, and they were protected by a strong calcareous skeleton. The animal had compound eyes on the upper surface of the head made of a large number of lenses, up to 15 000 in the genus *Remopleurides*. Some varieties originally bore several sets of antennae, but traces of these have only rarely been preserved. Sometimes the larva are found in fine-grained rocks and it has been possible to trace their life history and the development of the individual. The Upper Palaeolithic Magdalenian layer at the rock shelter site of 'Grotte du Trilobite' (Arcy-sur-Cure, Yonne, France) yielded a Silurian trilobite, perforated for suspension, together with a carving of a beetle made in lignite. Both were perforated for suspension by a pair of holes drilled through the lateral grooves, and it is tempting to suppose that the craftsmen visualised the trilobite as a kind of beetle, and then tried to carve another to match it. Certainly the two objects are very similar in form. Trilobites must surely be the most striking and beautiful of all fossils. The particular species recorded from this site is *Dalmanites hawlei*, which is not found in any French rocks but comes from southern Germany, 1250 miles (2000 km) to the east, so a trade route of some variety seems possible. Man's fondness for the beetle shape recurs later in time with the popular scarabs (p. 112) generally carved in that form.

Figure 2 (p. 22) shows the stages in the gradual evolution of life, beginning during the pre-Cambrian, a period which lasted a total of some 4500 million years (at least nine-tenths of the total age of the earth); fossils from this period are very rare indeed. Lime-secreting algae are, however, found in pre-Cambrian deposits of anthracite and limestone, forming indirect evidence for the existence of life. Primitive algae and fungi were also recorded from the cherts of western England, but animal fossils of any kind are very rare. In the succeeding Cambrian, fossils are much more widespread including algae, arthropods, brachiopods, sponges, worms, molluscs and echinoids, all of which lived in the sea. The Ordovician saw the appearance of new groups together with the oldest vertebrates, and in the Silurian the first plants appear. The oldest recorded land plants come from upper Silurian rocks in Australia, although even earlier finds have been tentatively suggested from elsewhere. Some of the best-preserved fossils, including fish, come from ancient reefs in Silurian limestones. The Devonian saw an expansion in the diversity of fishes, together with the appearance of the first primitive amphibians, sharks and jawless fish. The oldest spiders, millipedes and insects also appeared at this time, as did freshwater bivalves. The early plants lacked true roots and leaves, but later in the Devonian great forests of scale-trees and seed-ferns flourished while in some areas thick deposits of red sands and muds accumulated. In the Carboniferous life was so abundant that the plants and animals living in the shallow warm seas sometimes make up the bulk of the rocks. On land it was the time of the great coal forests in low-lying swampy areas, teeming with giant insects and amphibians. During the Permian the coal forest plants were replaced by primitive conifers and new forms of reptiles developed, which in the succeeding Mesozoic were to overshadow all other forms of animals as well as some of the new invertebrate forms. Ammonites lived in great numbers in the seas, and birds, mammals and many modern insects appeared. Elm, oak, maple and other broadleaved trees became common, the development of some of the new forms of flowering plants depending on the parallel development of insects which pollinated the flowers. Landform changes included vast new mountain ranges being pushed up, and alterations of the general configuration of land and sea. Triassic rocks resemble those of the Permian, thick sequences of red shales and sandstones deposited in temporary lakes, deserts and basins. The first dinosaurs appeared and later established mastery. In the seas new types of sponges and protozoans developed, gastropods and lamellibranchs flourished. The succeeding Jurassic, named after the Jura mountains, is the true age of the dinosaurs, together with flying reptiles, carnivorous icthyosaurs in the seas and great ammonites, some up to 6 ft (2 m) in diameter. Archaeopteryx, the oldest known bird, is found at this time. Cyclads (tree-ferns), conifers, ferns and ginkgos were common among the plants, one species of the latter surviving to the present day. The succeeding Cretaceous period is named after its most characteristic formation, the

Chalk, and lasted for some seventy million years. Vast thicknesses of marine and continental sediments marked major advances and recessions of the sea and at the end of the period earth movements produced the ranges which are now the Andes and the Rocky mountains. The Cretaceous is the last period in the Mesozoic, and the most significant new arrivals were the flowering plants, which helped the spread of mammals by providing new food sources. Dinosaurs were still common and the mammals as yet insignificant, but their remains included two groups which were new, the oppossum-like pouched marsupial and the insectivores, forerunners of the shrews. The life forms of the Cenozoic (Tertiary era) are more familiar to us, since many have survived into the present day without drastic change. It was a period when the hitherto omnipotent reptiles and amphibians became inconspicuous, and the fauna was dominated by mammals. Great phases of mountain building and volcanic activity took place, and at the extreme end of the era the first steps along the road to man were finally taken. During the lower Tertiary (Palaeocene, Eocene, Oligene) thick marine beds in the basins of London, Paris and Hampshire were formed, and there was much volcanic activity in central Europe and in Scotland. The life of the period was typified by mammals, ancestral rodents and primates, and in Eocene times more advanced forms of mammals included the early horses, the giant pig and mastodons. Mountain building took place as a result of great crustal disturbances in the Alps, Carpathians, Pyrenees, Apennines, Himalayas and parts of North America. The Upper Tertiary (comprising the Miocene and Pliocene) is marked by the continuous evolution of modern mammals. Continental uplift eventually resulted in the production of drier climates and converted the widespread lowland forests into grazing prairies. This resulted in the evolution of new mammal types associated with the change from browsing to grazing, and was probably one of the determining factors in the evolution of the first hominids. The Quaternary era is the time of the great Ice Age, comprising a complex sequence of alternating cold and warm periods corresponding with the movements of the ice sheet. These formed a backcloth to the gradual development of modern man, which occupied at least three million years from the appearance of the first hominids to the arrival of *Homo sapiens*. The succeeding few millennia in which are found all the developments of culture are but a second in time in comparison with what had gone before.

CHAPTER 2

Tools, weapons and artefacts

'There is nothing useless in nature; not even uselessness itself'

Montaigne

The fossil records of the human race and its tools are so closely linked that until recently the archaeological discovery of tools was considered sufficient evidence to deduce the presence of *Homo sapiens*, although it is now clear that tools antedate the earliest known *Homo sapiens*. It has even been proposed that the correct name for our species should be *Homo faber* (the maker of tools) because of the way in which we connect ourselves so closely with our artefacts. Toolmaking was one of the most important factors in the evolution of culture, and new archaeological evidence suggests that it was also of primary importance in our physical evolution. Indeed it was Charles Darwin himself who first suggested that tool use is both the cause and the effect of bipedal locomotion. Walking on two legs leaves the hands free to play with sticks and stones, and later to modify them, and the advantages gained from having these objects lead to more bipedalism and more tool use. The possession of a stone tool gives immense benefits to its owner. It can be held in the hand for pounding, digging or scraping, used as a weapon, a tool for cutting meat or a fabricator for other materials.

The earliest attempts at tool making, as opposed to tool using, seem to be associated with remains of the hominid *Homo habilis*, first discovered in Olduvai Gorge, Tanzania. This feature is an offshoot of the Great Rift valley, about 300 ft (90 m) deep and developed in stratified deposits including lavas and sedimentary rocks of both aeolian and lacustrine facies. Bed 1, which contained the remains of *Homo habilis*, is made of volcanic tuff, and dated to at least one and a half million years ago. It lies at the base of the sequence directly upon basalt lava from the neighbouring volcanoes. The makers of the tools, upright, bipedal hominids, with brains only half the size of ours, probably also had rudimentary houses. A rough circle of loosely piled stones was discovered which it is thought might have been the basis for some form of windbreak. The next layer at Olduvai, Bed 2, is more varied in composition and includes waterlain material, wind deposits, redeposited tuffs and several distinct archaeological layers, with additional types of stone tool.

These first tools, forming part of the Oldowan culture, were crudely made by chipping off some flakes from one or both sides of a lava, quartzite or vein-quartz pebble to give a sharp edge, using another stone as a hammer. It is salutary to reflect that such pebble tools constitute man's principal technological adaptation for a period at least fifty times as long as recorded history. Later in time tool making techniques improved, tool edges becoming more regular and the worked area extended to occupy more of the surface of the tool. Later still handaxes were shaped by using hammers of soft materials (such as wood, bone or antler) to produce a more durable edge and thinner tools. The all-purpose handaxe which developed from the chopping tool was to remain, together with struck flakes, the only tool available to early hominids for a period of not less than a million years. Some groups clearly preferred to use choppers rather than axes, but in Europe it is possible to see a gradual progression from the very first thick crudely made handaxes to the thin, elegant, refined models used some three-quarters of a million years later. Developments included the refinement of the use of flakes to make a complete tool-kit (saws, borers,

1

2

3

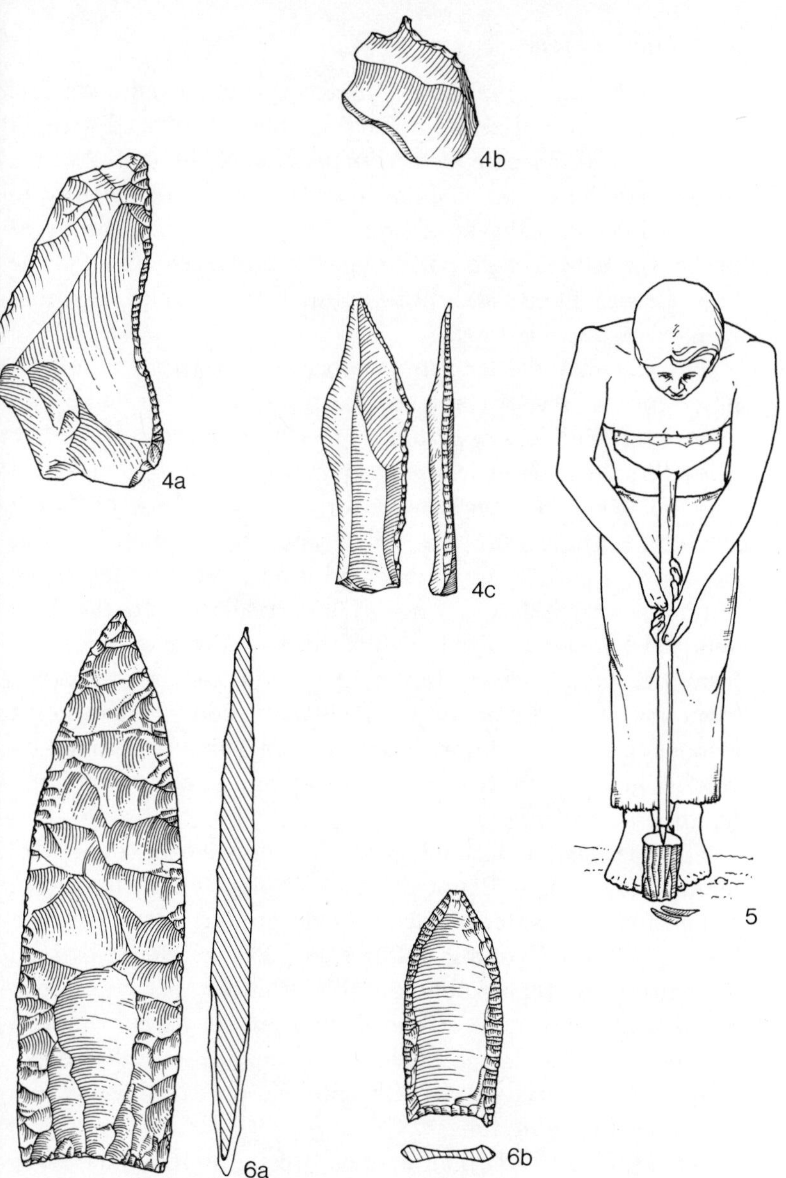

Figure 7. Techniques for the manufacture of stone tools. (1) Direct percussion with a hammerstone, to make a chopping tool. (2) Flaking with a soft hammer to make a handaxe. (3) Pressure flaking: the hand which is holding the tool is covered by leather, and held against the left knee; the right knee adds power to the hand which retouches by striking off minute flakes. (4) Some Mousterian tool-types: (a) a side-scraper, (b) a small borer, (c) a backed knife, (5) chest-punch technique for making long blades, (6) Palaeo-Indian implements from America: (a) Clovis point, (b) Folsom point.

knives and scrapers) of the sort used by Neanderthal man. The development of pressure flaking enabled a high degree of control to be exerted over the final shape of the tool. As time progressed the clumsy handaxes and flake tools gave way to blades, long thin slivers of stone more than twice as long as broad. Stone tool-making techniques are, of course, used as the basis for classifying Palaeolithic cultures, the principal divisions being shown in Figure 7.

The raw material for European stone industries was usually flint, since it is very common, has a conchoidal fracture and gives a very satisfactory cutting edge. Chert (a micro-crystalline silica which occurs in sedimentary rocks) was also used, but it does not seem to have been so satisfactory because of its flat fracture. Outside Europe a wider range of raw materials was exploited, especially quartzites and other metamorphic rocks, but flint was preferred when it was available. In the New World, where the establishment of the existence of an early prehistory is comparatively recent, the commonest raw material was obsidian, and many of the tools were produced by using a wooden punch to obtain flakes from a core, sometimes involving heavy pressure exerted by leaning the chest on a long-handled punch (Fig. 7).

The last major technological development in stone tool manufacture was undoubtedly the art of polishing the stone, using sand and water to give a finely ground edge. This is a feature of many Neolithic cultures, and axes produced by such methods were remarkably durable, sharper than primitive metal blades but more brittle. Even after the advent of metal working, flint tools continued to be made, and the art of knapping has survived virtually into the present day because of the need for gun-flints.

The influence of fashion is often grossly underestimated by typology-orientated archaeologists, not least when considering stone tools. The objects which survive are the results not only of the choice of raw materials and the competence of the craftsmen but also of less concrete factors such as the climate of opinion at the time, or the whim of a particular patron. The utilisation of one class of raw materials at the expense of another, apparently equally suitable for the purpose, may have such a relatively simple explanation. Qualities admired in the present artistic and economic climate include sturdiness, resistance to wear, simplicity of design and, primarily, cheapness. The ritual element in the production of a simple object is no longer of importance, and new concepts have been introduced, such as built-in obsolescence. Similar factors, the evidence for which has not, of course, survived, probably always conditioned the choice of raw materials for artefacts. Thus a particular type of material or shape of tool might go out of fashion very quickly, or might re-appear in a slightly different form in another culture at a totally different time, like the Regency use of Egyptian-style cane and ebony furniture. Objects manufactured during any particular period seldom provide a datum line with the reliability that 'zone fossils' do for geological time, because the unpredictable human element must always be taken into consideration. The linear typological series so prevalent until recently has given ground before the school of archaeologists who are paying more attention to the limitations of their evidence.

The existence of a resource in an area does not mean that it will necessarily be used. In prehistoric times the population of a region must have been acquainted with absolutely everything that it could offer in terms of exploitable materials, but it does not necessarily follow that they could or wished to exploit them. This is seen particularly clearly in terms of metallic minerals. Occasionally, in societies which had no knowledge of the smelting or casting of copper, lumps of copper are used as ornaments, without any regard for the nature of the metal. Before the smiths had discovered how to obtain the high temperatures required for the smelting of iron any amount of bog iron ore (limonite) or meteoritic iron could go unremarked. The latter material did, however, form one of the earliest exploited sources of iron, and the dagger in the 14th century BC tomb of Tutankhamun was probably made of this material.

A technologically complex society will favour certain classes of raw material at the expense of others, as well as adapting the raw material to the job in hand. The pattern of resource exploitation will vary both with its availability and workability, with technological progress and geographical location, as well as with such vital factors as social patterning or the degree of manpower control.

In the past cultural contact has been principally demonstrated by typological similarities between artefacts, but many such comparisons are open to discussion and differences of opinion. This is why the study of raw materials imported and used in places far from their origin is of such importance. It is necessary to study the properties of the specimen which are characteristic of material from a particular source, thus making it possible to assign artefacts to their source locations. A great deal of attention has been focused in recent years on the petrological examination of British Neolithic axes in the 3rd millennium BC to help determine early trade routes and shed some light on the Neolithic economy. The results have been published as a series of regional reports, locating the axe-making factories and then plotting distribution maps for their products. Work has been concentrated on axes made from materials other than flint or chert, and a series of some twenty distinct groups has been isolated, utilising a range of very diverse materials. The best known of the groups are undoubtedly the axes of Group VI, made from the volcanic tuffs found in the Langdale area of the Lake District; Group VII, from a porphyritic microdiorite located at Graig Lwyd, near Penmaenmawr (North Wales); and Group XX made from coarse sandy tuff found in the Charnwood forest area of Leicestershire. The distribution patterns of the axe factory products are very varied, a few having clearly been producing only for the local market, while others had a very much wider distribution, being extensively traded hundreds of miles away.

One study considered the relationships between archaeological artefact distributions and their production, marketing and distribution centres. Several groups of artefacts were examined where adequate samples were available. These including two of the Neolithic axe groups, axes from Group I, produced at a source near Penzance in Cornwall, and Group

VI, from the Langdale factory, chosen since they have been the subject of particularly detailed distribution studies. Analysis showed that the Neolithic axe production of Cornwall was rather a small concern which did not flood the market near the source, but the products travelled a long way by sea and are found as far afield as Yorkshire and East Anglia. The axes from the Langdale factory, on the other hand, are found over a much more extensive area, and seem to have completely flooded the market near the source, although the two factories are at least partly contemporary. The large size of this production concern is reflected in the widespread distribution of the axe rough-outs. The size of the production area was taken as the distance from the factory to the farthest point at which the rough-outs are found, and there seems to be a statistically predictable 'breaking point' corresponding quite well to the actual boundary between the two trade areas. North of a line drawn roughly between Bristol and Brighton the Group VI (Langdale) axes are more common, and south of it the Group I axes have a virtual monopoly. The great ritual centre of Avebury in Wiltshire seems to have been 'the capital emporium of the whole axe trade of the country', and it is situated significantly on the 'breaking point' between two major trade areas.

British Neolithic axes also include a group made of jade, the name used for two distinct minerals, jadeite (a pyroxene) and nephrite (an amphibole). All but two of the British axes are made of jadeite and they tend to be of a triangular shape with a pointed butt and a gently curved cutting edge. Some, of a clear green colour, are objects of outstanding beauty, and over seventy-five examples have now been discovered. An especially splendid find from the Somerset levels has recently been published: an axe some 8 in (203 mm) long with a smooth highly polished surface and unblemished edge, associated with a wooden track-way radiocarbon dated to around 3200 BC. The source of the jadeite is as yet unknown, but probably to be found on the Continent. One authority has suggested the possibility of cycles of gifts being exchanged in Neolithic Europe, stone axes forming one of the major traded items. Such a beautiful object seems unlikely to have been intended for mundane wood chopping, and the jade axes may well have been prestige gifts or made especially for ceremonial purposes. The Maoris, who also worked with jade, took at least 100 man-hours to produce such an axe, and it seems improbable that such effort or such precious stone would be expended on a domestic artefact. Jade axes are also found on the mainland of Europe although the majority of battle-axes are of basalt, and in later time they are made to patterns which clearly imitate metal. Some particularly splendid examples of jadeite battle-axes were found in a treasure hoard at Borodino in Russia, probably dating from the 15th century BC (Fig. 8). The battle-axes are of the most graceful shapes, and were accompanied by mace heads, also of rare stone, including alabaster, and by silver spearheads with attractive gold inlay ornament. Such panoply is magnificent in its impracticality, and was clearly not designed for use. Further manifestations of this trend appear in the British Wessex cultures (2nd millennium BC),

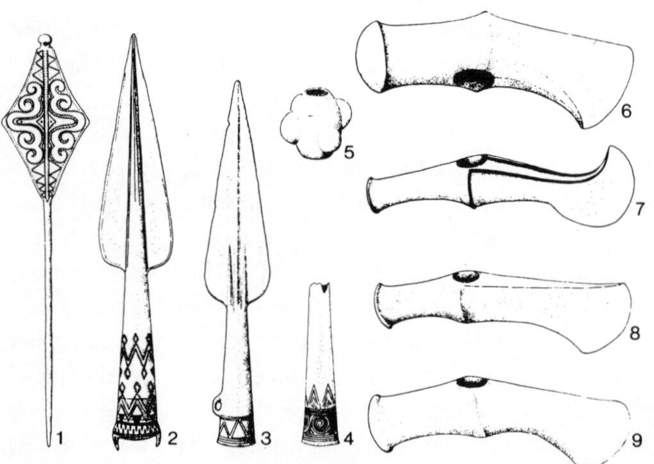

Figure 8. Part of the Borodino hoard, mid-second millennium BC, from south Russia: (1) silver pin, (2)–(4) silver spear heads with gold ornament, (5) alabaster mace head, (6)–(9) Jadeite battle axes, copying metal forms. Reproduced by kind permission of Professor S. Piggott and Edinburgh University Press.

Figure 9. A pair of jade pendants in the shape of symmetrically paired dragons. Fourth or early 3rd century BC, Ch'u tomb, Hopei, China. Reproduced by kind permission of Times Newspapers Ltd and Robert Harding Associates.

with weapons of fine stone, gold and jet, and in the later European Iron Age where some of the finds of Celtic armour had clearly been designed for ceremonial rather than actual battle.

The art of carving jade was particularly popular in China, and was carried to its greatest heights in the 5th and 4th centuries BC, the 'Period of the Warring States'. The motifs used seem to be related to those fashionable for bronze objects at the same period, the execution of the complex openwork designs being facilitated by improved sawing techniques and the use of a rapidly rotating drill. Double dragons and spirals were much esteemed as patterns, and Figure 9 shows two jade pendants, carved in openwork in the shape of symmetrically paired dragons. These were excavated in 1965 from a tomb of Ch'u (6th century BC), at Chiang-ling (Hopei, north-east China), which was near the early capital of the Ch'u state.

The Maya, whose culture flourished during the first millennium BC in Central America, also made fine jade carvings, including beautifully engraved rings very similar in design to the Chinese *pi*, sometimes used as toggles or ear-rings and often engraved with glyphs. The Aztecs also made jade and porphyry models and figurines, a difficult task demanding craftsmen skilled in the working of such hard materials, but many of the finest pieces were smashed by the Spanish after the conquest. Jade was a highly prized substance among the Aztecs and, together with gold and silver, usually reserved for religious ornaments. Stealing it was punishable by death. Both jadeite and nephrite occur in the New World but the American variety is easily distinguishable from the Asian. The conquistador Bernal Diáz told a story of the night when Cortés reached Mexico City, then the Aztec capital, and after taking his share of the treasure turned the rest over to his troops. Many were burdened with quantities of gold and later drowned in the numerous canals which surrounded the city, but Diáz himself, who had studied the Aztec values, took only four jade objects which he was later able to exchange for medical attention and food. In response to the demands of the Spanish invaders for objects of value the Aztecs offered jade and turquoise, rather than the gold which the Spaniards wanted but which the Aztecs did not value so highly.

Apart from flint the most common raw material for the manufacture of tools and weapons is obsidian, which Pliny said was named after a certain Obsius, who found it in Ethiopia. It is formed when certain sorts of silica-rich volcanic lava cool in circumstances which prevent crystal formation. Not all sorts of volcanic lava will produce it and with exposure to weathering and the hot groundwaters common in volcanic areas it becomes completely dehydrated and loses its conchoidal fracture, later ending completely crystalline. Obsidian closely resembles black glass, and was also used in antiquity for mirrors, the earliest examples of which are found set in plaster, from the Anatolian Neolithic site of Çatal Hüyük (6500–5650 BC). Its primary use has, however, always been for weapons, although it was periodically fashionable as a gemstone and has even been used for the carving of statues.

Obsidian has a conchoidal (shell-like) fracture in the same

way as flint, breaking to give a curved and concentrically ribbed surface. It is found in many, but not all, regions of volcanic activity, and there are at least twenty-five distinct sources recognised in the Mediterranean area alone. Other sources include East Africa, New Zealand, North America, Mexico, Japan and Iceland, all of which were utilised in prehistoric times. Obsidian sources and tools in the Mediterranean have recently been the subject of a series of characterisation studies, with similar objectives to those of the project involving Neolithic axes, but using a different series of techniques. The relatively small number of sources makes such characterisation worthwhile, since if there had been too many it would have been impossible, as is largely the case with flint sources, certainly in the Palaeolithic period before flint was obtained by mining. It was therefore possible to assign a place of origin to an excavated obsidian artefact by analysing its properties and comparing them with the properties of obsidian in the source areas. The study involves finding a set of properties which are the same, or nearly the same, in specimens from the same source, and which differ noticeably in obsidians from different sources. The first step in the process is to test the properties of the material obtained from a single source. This was tried by working from hand specimens and then from thin sections, both of which turned out to be unsatisfactory since no systematic variation between areas could be found. In an early paper dealing with this problem optical spectrography was used to distinguish the proportions of trace elements present (elements present in the rock in proportions between .0001% and 1%). Quantitative values for sixteen elements were determined, and on this basis the whole sample studied (from natural sources and archaeological sites in the Mediterranean area) was divided into six major groups. It was then possible to relate artefacts to source area, which solved a number of archaeological problems, for example by diagnosing the source of the obsidian used by the Neolithic temple builders of Malta, as the islands of Pantelleria (off the Tunisian coast) and Lipari (near Sicily). Further analysis of obsidian in the Near East, based on fairly small quantities found at much earlier prehistoric sites, illustrated the fact that although such organised trade certainly did exist in Upper Palaeolithic times, it was preceded by the nomadic hunting bands obtaining obsidian from small-scale exchanges between groups or individuals, such as those documented in recent times among Australian Aborigines. During Neolithic times more organised systems of supply and exchange began, and by the Bronze Age it is possible to imagine specialist merchants, using pack animals (such as the donkey) for short distances, and foot traffic (probably slaves) for longer hauls. Evidence has been found to support the existence of marine traffic in obsidian on the Mediterranean from the 6th millennium BC, taking Melos obsidian to the early Neolithic sites of the Greek mainland and Crete, and trading along the Levantine coast.

From the Bronze Age onwards written records are available to illustrate the existence of very well-used trade routes in various commodities, such as the Assyrian documents recording well-organised trade between the Assyrian colony at Kultepe in Cappadocia, and their Mesopotamian homeland. Donkeys were used to carry copper, tin and other raw materials from Cappadocia, returning with textiles. Documentary evidence also exists for similar trade in the Persian Gulf, merchants from Ur taking silver, oil, garments and wool to Telmun (Bahrein) and returning with copper, gold, ivory, wood, lapis lazuli and other such exotic products. Although obsidian was not an especially important commodity at so late a date it seems likely that it was traded along similar networks. Workers in this field stress that the very early radiocarbon dates available for the obsidian trade illustrate early paths for cultural contact, and exchange of information, which must have contributed in no small way to the technological and cultural advances of the period which is often described as the 'Neolithic Revolution'. This proven trade in artefact raw material makes it easier to see paths for the diffusion of ideas, and illustrates the fact that inter-culture contact at an early date was far more widespread than had hitherto been supposed.

Obsidian was also widely traded in the New World, and it was the raw material used by Aztecs for projectile points, sharp as razors and superbly made. Obsidian flakes and blades were also handy for engraving designs on pottery. Notched blades of scalpel-like thinness made arrowheads, and the same material was carved into figurines and little amulets finished to a mirror-like smoothness, and the obsidian eyes of the great idols. Spears and wooden clubs were set with pressure-flaked obsidian blades which led to the development of a body armour made from quilted cotton coated in strong brine, which covered the whole body rather like a suit of combinations. This provided excellent protection against obsidian-tipped arrows, and was even adopted by the Spanish Conquistadores as being lighter and cooler than steel armour. Flint, although sometimes used for the manufacture of stone tools, was not nearly so popular. Aztec metal technology was poor in contrast to their expertise in the working of stone, and obsidian was at least as effective for tools and weapons as their edged metal objects. Ceremonial blood-letting ritual called for a constant supply of thin pressure-flaked blades, yet the skill of the workmen was such that the same brittle material could be turned into vases and mirrors. The latter, however, are very rarely found, and it is thought that their sole use was for ritualistic magic rather than domestic purposes. Blocks of obsidian were sometimes polished to give deliberately weird reflections, and lumps of pyrites also used in the same way. Pyrite flakes also occur set in mosaics, glued to wood and shell backings. One mirror is known made of marcasite, the surface ground in such a way that a magnified reflection is obtained.

Marcasite (iron sulphide, FeS_2), is a mineral found in low-temperature near-surface deposits in sedimentary rocks, formed as a result of the segregation of iron-bearing minerals. It is chemically identical with pyrite (Fe_2S) but distinct in its crystalline form. When distinctly formed crystals are not to be observed, as in the commonly occurring nodular masses with internal radiating structure, it is almost impossible to distinguish between marcasite and pyrite. It is an uncommon substance in archaeological contexts, although there is a find of a small hemispherical cup, about 1¾ in. (45 mm) in diameter, associated with a Middle Bronze Age burial at Simonston cairn, in South Wales. It has been produced from an almost spherical nodule of marcasite, which must have come from an outcrop of the Chalk, at least fifty miles away. The cup was found in association with the bones of a child, still in possession of its milk teeth, and the excavator put forward the theory that it had been a toy.

Other substances, apart from obsidian and marcasite, which were used in antiquity to make mirrors include black varieties of mica, such as lepidomelane. Mica is one of the group of minerals especially distinguished by their ready cleavage into thin plates. They consist of aluminium silicates with compounds of iron, magnesium, potassium or sodium, and are found plentifully in granites and gneiss. Mica mirrors are found in archaic times in northern Asia and small flakes of mica were used as sequins, some of which turn up in the Egyptian colony of Middle Kingdom (19th century BC) at Kerma, in the Sudan, where they seem to have been used for decorating caps. Mica flakes were strewn on the surface of the Circus Maximus during the Games at Rome, to give an attractive sparkling effect. The substance is sometimes found included in pottery, and it seems that micaceous clays were selected in the (erroneous) belief that the mica content would be conducive to a good gloss. There is a distinctive imported micaceous sub-type of Roman tableware, found at a number of important military sites in Britain, such as Silchester and Caerleon. The mica in the clays occurs in the form of tiny platelets, but the clay was far from being a satisfactory raw material. The distinctive appearance has, however, assisted ceramicists in plotting the distribution of the form.

Potting clays and ceramics should, technically, be considered here, but they are of such archaeological importance that their study has become a subject in its own right. This is a result of the evidence that pottery changes very little as a result of burial, even if the original vessels are found only as fragments, or as collections of potsherds. Pottery preserves both its design and physical properties and, being cheap and simple to make, was often produced in large quantities by relatively primitive societies. Pottery vessels are almost infinitely variable, since the raw material, form, decoration and temper represent the personal preferences of the potter or his clients. Potsherds therefore constitute a direct reflection, in a virtually unchanged form, of the skills and ideas of ancient peoples.

In the past prehistorians tended to assume that all pottery was made for domestic purposes from raw materials available near the home. Prehistoric trade in pottery was thought to be minimal, since pots, being of low intrinsic value, would have been scarcely worth the effort involved in trade. Pottery styles tended to be localised both in space and time, and it was quite common to find entire periods and cultures distinguished solely on the basis of changes in their ceramic forms. This assumption is now being challenged by the application of objective scientific techniques, particularly those of petrofabric and 'heavy' mineral analysis, which have shed a great deal of light on the study of prehistoric pottery trade, showing it to be much more extensive and better organised than had formerly been supposed. This has initiated a reconsideration of archaeological deduction based on ceramic evidence.

Various mineral substances were also used as coating for pottery, or in slips, washes, glazes and other decoration. Graphite painting on pottery is known from Chalcolithic farming villages in the Balkans, and also in the Czech Iron Age. Graphite, a soft, black form of carbon, is found particularly in crystalline limestones, and in metamorphic rocks. It usually contains from 3 to 50% clay, together with other impurities, and is of course used today on a large scale in the manufacture of pencils. Haematite (Fe_2O_3), a red ore of iron, was also used as a decorative coating for pottery, and is particularly common in the early British Iron Age and on the Continent at the same period.

Throughout history there seem to have been a certain number of other mineral substances which were almost exclusively reserved by early societies for religious or ceremonial use. Jade, mentioned above, is one of these, and others are alabaster, rock crystal and turquoise, all of which are far from common and of outstandingly attractive appearance. Alabaster is a compact, crystalline calcareous rock, white or yellowish white in colour and transluscent in thin section. It occurs in thick beds of the mineral gypsum ($CaSO_4.2H_2O$) and, owing to its softness, lends itself to carving. Occasionally the term alabaster is wrongly used for transluscent masses of calcium carbonate ($CaCO_3$) which is harder. Alabaster was a favoured Egyptian raw material for vases, mace heads and sarcophagi, for example those of the pharaohs Hetepheres (4th Dynasty) and Seti I. A particularly fine specimen of inlaid alabaster is seen in the canopic chest of Tutankhamun, made of first quality material incised with hieroglyphics stained with a black pigment, the inscription evoking the words pronounced by each of the four goddesses carved in relief on the four corners of the chest. Egypt was one of the main sources of alabaster for the Roman world, where it was used first of all only for drinking cups, but later, after supplies became more plentiful, for monumental architecture, especially for the construction of columns. Pliny says that the name comes from *alabastra*, little jars shaped like amphorae without handles, used for holding perfumes. The Greek word ἀλάβαστος is generally taken to mean a globular vase without a handle, used for the same purpose, but not necessarily made of alabaster. The substance is referred to by many classical writers, including Herodotus and Theophrastus, who mention 'calcareous alabaster'. The Greek ἀλάβαστοθήκη means either a case of small alabaster ornaments or a small box or casket. A New Testament reference to the use of alabaster comes in the story of Mary Magdalene, who had 'an alabaster box of ointment', which she used to anoint the feet of Jesus. It is interesting to note that the box was seemingly of negligible value compared to the ointment, the alabaster being chosen simply for its physical properties and presumably for its attractive appearance, rather than for any rarity value. Larger boxes were often made of ornamental stones such as marble, and these could even be used as lethal weapons, as is shown by the sad demise of Constantine III in AD 668, murdered by his bath attendant Andrea who hit him on the head with a marble soapbox.

Steatite (soapstone), a massive variety of talc, was also sometimes used to make boxes, although it is rather soft. Its softness and pleasant white or grey colour made it very suitable for carving into small objects such as amulets, beads and scarabs. It had the additional advantage of being infusible, which made it a good basis for glazing, and it may be heated without decomposition or fracture, resulting in a product hard enough to scratch glass. Glazed steatite was rather popular in Egypt until the Arab period, and many of the modern forgeries of scarabs and other antiquities hawked to unprotesting tourists are made of this material.

The Greeks, and later the Romans utilised rock crystal for the manufacture of cups and vases, believing it to be hardened ice (the word κρύσταλλος *crystallos* in Greek means 'clear-ice'). It must have provided a useful source of income for the unscrupulous, since it could be stained to imitate coloured gems, but Pliny refused to give the recipe in case it was followed. When, in AD 68, Nero received a message saying that all was lost, and that the new emperor (Galba) was marching on Rome with the support of all the legions, he broke two crystal drinking vessels, reputedly priceless, in a final outburst of rage. The substance was very highly valued, as the following quotation illustrated, 'Rock crystal provides yet another example of a crazy addiction, for not many years ago a respectable married woman, who was by no means rich, paid 150 000 sesterces for a single dipper' (Pliny 37.28). This would be equivalent to at least £20 000 in the present day, but one wonders, from the note of censure, whether such a purchase would have been less reprehensible if carried out by a spinster. Rock crystal seems to have been used only for containers for cold drinks, since it cannot withstand heat. It was also used for vases and amphorae, one of which was described by Xenocrates as having a capacity of six gallons. Pieces of rock crystal appear in many cultures used as gemstones, and the Minoans especially made great use of it for vases and ornaments. There is one famous find of an exquisite rock crystal sprinkler, from the great Cretan palace of Kato Zakro, dated to 1500 BC.

Fluorspar or fluorite (CaF_2) is another popular mineral used for the manufacture of expensive luxury goods. Like rock crystal it is its fragility as well as intrinsic beauty which renders it so costly. Ultimate luxury lies in the possession of an expensive object which can be totally destroyed in a second. When the ex-consul Titus Petronius was facing death he broke, to spite Nero, a single myrrhine (fluorspar) dipper worth 300 000 sesterces (£40 000). Nero, however, outdid him by paying 1 million sesterces (£133 000) for a single bowl made from the same material. Fluorspar objects often also have a pleasant smell, due to the resin in which they are soaked to prevent disintegration during working, and several fine specimens of bowls made by this method are on display in the Geological Museum in London. In Britain the best quality fluorspar is the famous 'Blue John', veined purple and white in colour, mined in Derbyshire.

Turquoise is a basic hydrous phosphate of aluminium and copper, ($CuAl_6(PO_4)_4.(OH)_84H_2O$), blue to bluish-green in colour. It was extensively used in jewellery whenever it was available, and in the present day is still mined for that purpose in Iran, the United States (particularly New Mexico), Egypt and the USSR, from deposits in trachytes and certain other igneous rocks. It is frequently set in gold, which enhances the colour, but the stone is vulnerable to decay if brought into contact with liquids such as water, wine or vinegar. The most spectacular examples of turquoise work come from Mesoamerica, where the substance was highly prized by both Mixtecs and Aztecs, and was much used in jewellery and mosaics. Turquoise mosaics were known there even in pre-Classical times (around 1000 BC), and were then used primarily for ornamenting the handles of sacrificial knives and for the manufacture of masks and shields. The mosaics, which utilise materials of different types, are works of art unique in the world, and it is tragic that so few have survived. Figure 10 shows the so-called 'Eagle Knight' sacrificial knife, with a finely flaked stone blade (probably of Mixtec workmanship) and a wooden handle in the form of a crouching Eagle Knight, one of the Aztec warrior orders, inlaid with a mosaic of turquoise, shell and lignite. This beautiful object was used for human heart sacrifices, made by removing the hearts from living people in vast numbers, and offering them to the sun god. Twenty

Figure 10. Aztec 'Eagle Knight' knife. The handle is in the form of a crouching 'Eagle Knight', whose face is seen in the open beak of a head-dress in the form of an eagle's head, the wings covering his shoulders. The mosaic work is of turquoise, malachite, lignite and shell. The blade is honey-coloured chalcedony; length, 12½ in. (32 cm). Reproduced by kind permission of the Trustees of the British Museum, Department of Ethnography.

thousand people were popularly supposed to have been slaughtered for the festival marking the dedication of the last enlargement of the Aztec capital Tenochtitlan. Victims were sacrificed to provide human food to nourish the sun on his daily journey, and thus to prevent the world from coming to an end. Death in battle or on the sacrificial stone was the ultimate ambition of every warrior, since it would result in immediate elevation to the highest heaven. This theme of the celestial consolation prize is repeated in numerous societies, and even today the death of a soldier on active service calls forth admiration and a kind of quasi-religious awe which never accompanies those who die peacefully at home in their beds. Much of the Aztec art reflects the brutality of their religion, and many of the actual objects seem to have been made by craftsmen whose cultural origins lie with the Mixtecs, their predecessors. The mask in Figure 11 is made of a human skull encrusted with a mosaic of turquoise, lignite and shell, with eyes of iron pyrites. It represents the god Tezcatlipoca, and is one of the most spectacular manifestations of Aztec art.

Figure 11. Aztec mask, based on a human skull, thought to represent the god Tezcatlipoca. Turquoise and lignite mosaic, the inside of the mask covered with soft leather. The eyes are polished convex discs of iron pyrites set in white shell. Height 8 in. (20 cm). Reproduced by kind permission of the Trustees of the British Museum, Department of Ethnography.

CHAPTER 3

Bricks and mortar

'Σώματα πολλα τρέφειν, καὶ δώματα πόλλ 'ἀνεγέιρειν
ἀτραπὸς εἰʒ πενίιην ἐστὶν ἑτοιμοτάτη'

*(The Way to poverty
Keep open home; dabble in bricks and mortar
Of all the roads to ruin none is shorter)*

(Anon. Greek poet, trs. Wellesley)

It has often been suggested that houses built of mudbrick antedate the first proper stone constructions, but with the discovery of stone-built houses in the proto-Neolithic Natufian cultures (dated to between 9000 and 7000 BC) of the Near East, this can no longer be thought to be the case. There is no apparent chronological succession from mudbrick hut to stone palace, and while the former are exclusively confined to hot climates the converse is not necessarily true. Mudbricks are made by forming clay into lumps of suitable size, drying them in the sun and laying them in a wall using mud mortar. The bricks may be of almost any size, although use was sometimes made of a simple mould for standardisation. This method of wall construction was used by all the earliest urban societies for domestic buildings, stone being reserved for municipal projects such as temples, and for funerary monuments. The Neolithic peoples living at Jericho in the 7th millennium BC made their bricks with double rows of thumb impressions on the upper surface, presumably to act as 'keying' for the mortar. The finished wall was then covered with plaster, sometimes painted in bright colours, especially red. The size of the mudbricks used varies between cultures, and in Mesopotamia (ancient Iraq) bricks of up to 15 in. (38 cm) square and 4 in. (10 cm) thick were used for the construction of vast walls up to 20 ft (6 m) in thickness. These enormous structures, dating from 2000 to 700 BC, were often encased in burnt brick set in bitumen as a protection, although in at least one case (the town of Erech), the ziggurat (tower) had its outer surface protected by thousands of pieces of pottery, pressed into the brickwork while it was still slightly plastic. In Egypt sun-dried mudbricks were used for all domestic building until Roman times, when the kiln was introduced. Such brick building was, of course, only suitable for a hot dry country, and sun-dried bricks would rapidly disintegrate in the more temperate climate of Europe. The maximum life span of a mudbrick building is not precisely known, but from counting the successive annual coats of plaster it has been estimated at less than twenty years. After the buildings collapsed a new one was often erected on the debris, a process which resulted in the gradual aggradation of a town or village, until the latest houses were standing on artificial hills, known as *tells*. Such mounds are found widely all over the Near and Middle East, and as far west as Greece and the Balkans. The depth of a tell may be very great, as at Karanovo in Bulgaria where 40 ft (12.2 m) of deposit has accumulated, covering a time span of some 4000 years. The houses are of a size suitable for a single family, and it has been estimated that a maximum of 300 people could have been living on the site at any one time. Egyptian bricks were made of Nile alluvium, basically clay and sand with small amounts of impurities. The plastic and cohesive properties depend on the relative proportions of the constituents of the mixture. Too much clay will mean that the bricks will shrink and eventually crack, and clay-rich sediments must be mixed with clay or chopped straw, which is also conversely added as a binder if the proportion of clay is low. It requires some skill to judge the precise quantity of additive needed to make perfect bricks, although the task of brick making must of necessity have been extremely boring and repetitive. We have an excellent description of the use of straw in brick making in the Old Testament, where Pharaoh (Rameses II, 13th century BC) vents his spite on the Israelites by forcing them to make bricks with no straw, and then accusing them of idleness when they were unable to supply the full daily quota (Exodus). Such bricks were sun dried in wooden moulds, exactly as they are today.

Many different types of clay were used for making bricks, the best being alluvial wind-blown sediments containing up to 30% sand and silt, the sand reducing the amount of shrinkage which occurs when the bricks are fired. The colour and texture of fired brick depends both on the impurities present in the clay, and on the conditions of firing. In Iraq and Iran very silty clay was used, containing fluviatile material from the Tigris and Euphrates together with blown sand and limestone dust, the latter giving the bricks their characteristic cream or beige colour. The red colour of the majority of bricks is made by firing the clay at between 900 and 1000°C in an oxidising atmosphere. Above this temperature the bricks become darker, purple or brown, and at temperatures above 1200°C grey bricks will be produced. In a reducing atmosphere (without oxygen) purple, brown or bluish bricks with black cores will result. Vegetable matter in brickmaking clay will burn black in firing, and if the kiln temperature is raised too fast a red skin is formed sealing in the carbon, a condition very common in early pottery.

Decorative brickwork was common at a later period in the East, the bricks often bearing patterns of coloured glazes, sometimes with the name of a particular king, the record of an important event or information relating to the construction of the building. In many cases the bricks were set in bitumen for added strength. Neither the Greeks nor Romans favoured decorative brickwork, their more florid architectural flourishes being carried out in stone. Particularly impressive examples of decorative brickwork come from Byzantine churches, including the early Christian churches at Ravenna. Bricks were chosen for their colour and cut to the desired shapes, a pleasing polychrome effect being obtained. If the zenith of this art occurs at Ravenna its nadir is certainly to be found in England, where the hideous buildings of Royal Holloway College in London or Keble College at Oxford exhibit Victorian decorative brickwork of surpassing, if magnificent, ugliness.

In the Roman world it was customary for each legion to have its own tile and brick kiln, at the main legionary base, the products bearing the legionary stamp. This habit of stamping tiles or bricks has been used both as a method for dating construction works, and for reconstructing troop movements. Some recent work has shown that it is, however, occasionally unwise to place too much emphasis on such evidence, which may quite easily be forged. At the Roman shore fort of Pevensey in Sussex some bricks or tiles were found stamped HON AUG ANDRIA, supposedly evidence for the refurbishing of the defences of the fort during the reign of the Emperor Honorius (AD 395–423). Only two of the stamped tiles were found, both of a fine hard grey fabric bearing traces of mortar. Examinations show that their fabric differed from that of the others still in the walls of Pevensey, and thermoluminescent dating suggested that they were made between 1900 and 1947. David Peacock concluded, on this basis, that the bricks were forgeries, possibly the work of Charles Dawson, a prime suspect in the case of the better-known Piltdown forgery.

The craft of tile making was carried to great heights in Medieval England, mainly as a result of the efforts of the Cistercian monks in the 13th century. They developed the 'encaustic' tile, which bore a pattern in raised relief. After the tile had hardened it was scraped down to the level of the original red body, leaving the pattern clear and distinct. Medieval floor tiles were often glazed, and generally combined into pictorial designs. Many fine examples are still to be seen in English churches, usually somewhat eroded by the feet of worshippers over several hundred years. Some especially fine tiles, depicting the miracles of Christ, survive in Ely Cathedral. After the Dissolution of the Monasteries tile making itself ceased in England until the 16th century, when majolica tiles became fashionable, chiefly as a result of influence and craft interchange with Holland. Indeed English tin glazed wares became known as Delft ware. A resurgence of the tiled floor fashion was seen on the plain red-tiled cottage floors, so popular a generation or so ago. Regrettably these have now gone out of fashion, principally due to the effort required to polish them, and have been replaced by patterned Continental-style ceramic tiles, part of every 'ideal home' kitchen decor.

Clay may also be used for the manufacture of terracotta (a word which literally means 'baked earth'). Terracotta products differ only from other ceramics such as pottery, brick or tile in their method of manufacture, since they are modelled or sculptured from carefully chosen clay, great care being taken to avoid distortion during firing. If the product is to be unglazed it is fired only once, if glazed it is fired twice. If the first firing is at a high temperature and the second, after the glaze has been applied, at a lower temperature, then the product is a form of faience (p. 112). The most suitable clays for the manufacture of terracotta are those that have been weathered, since this increases the plasticity and converts minerals such as iron pyrites into iron oxides, removes soluble salts, decomposes feldspars and micas and reduces alkalis. Weathered clay and grog (usually small pieces of fired clay, or sand) are mixed together, allowed to stand and then pressed into moulds. The firing is carefully controlled, done in an open kiln for unglazed wares and a ruffle kiln if a glaze is used. The process was much used in the ancient world, particularly by the Etruscans, for the production of small hand-modelled objects, such as statues, and for the manufacture of tiles and friezes using a baked clay mould. Greek roof tiles were often of terracotta, coloured by painting before the clay was fired. The Romans also made great use of the material, especially for wall panelling, which sometimes carries impressions of intaglios. In the Renaissance terracotta was also used for altar pieces, wall plaques and bas reliefs, and the Italian craftsman Torrigiano, a contemporary of Michelangelo, was commissioned by Henry VIII to make the exterior ornaments (crests and gargoyles) for the palace of Nonsuch. This high standard of craftsmanship in the material was never to be attained again, and later products, for example those used in the 19th and 20th century Gothic revival, do not come anywhere near the quality of the originals.

Mortar is the bonding material used for bedding and joining bricks or stonework. The most ancient variety was simply mud, but later gypsum (or lime) mortar was introduced. The difference between lime, mortar and plaster is one of degree only. In pre-Graeco-Roman times the Egyptians used clay for mortar with sun-dried brick, and gypsum mortar for use in stonework. The very earliest stone buildings seem, however, to have used mud mortar, and no finds of gypsum mortar are recorded from buildings erected before the reign of Ptolemy I (323–285 BC).

In Egyptian stonework the joints between the large blocks were so thin that the mortar acted more as a lubricant than a bonding material, helping the blocks to slide into position and providing some protection for the edges in case of damage in transit. Resin, strangely, was also sometimes used as a mortar, but not until Persian and Ptolemaic times. The Roman architect Vitruvius has many comments on the proper selection of the sand which must be mixed with lime for the mortar, stressing the need for it to be both clean and well washed. There is little real difference between the ingredients of mortar and concrete, although in the latter the aggregates which are added will be coarser.

Concrete was also used by the Romans, especially as a foundation or as a filling for walls made with stone blocks. *Opus incertum* was a facing of small stone blocks backed with concrete and *opus reticulatum* a wall of squared stones set on their sides at an angle of 45° to the horizontal, forming a netlike pattern. *Opus testaculum* (concrete walls filled with brick) was used from the 1st century BC until the end of the Western Empire, and from the 3rd century onwards stone and bricks were mixed with concrete to make *opus mixtum*. The Romans also used concrete in a more spectacular way for domes and vaults, for example the temple of Venus and Roma, at the east end of the Forum, dedicated by Hadrian in AD 135. In Britain an example of the Roman use of cement can be found at Verulamium (St Albans) where flints were placed in layers in wooden frameworks, with stiff mortar between the layers to reduce the pressure on the timbers.

Bitumen is a naturally occurring mixture of complex hydrocarbons, usually found in association with petroleum deposits. In the ancient world it was obtained from such reservoirs and used as a mortar, but today it forms one of the by-products of petroleum refining. Bitumen occurs principally in rock asphalt, of compositions varying from soft crystalline limestones with between 6 and 14% bitumen included, to massive crystalline limestones containing up to 20% bitumen. The largest known deposit is at Lake Trinidad in the West Indies, a fluid mixture of 50 to 60% bitumen and some silt, clay and insoluble organic matter. Similar deposits are found in Bermuda, Venezuela, Cuba and Texas. Bitumen also occurs as natural seepages over a wide area of the Middle East from Egypt to Pakistan, and its toughness was exploited by early peoples for lining drains, bonding brickwork and covering floors. Homes of the Al'Ubaid culture (*c.* 3500 BC) were made from a simple framework of arched bundles of reeds to which rush matting coated with bitumen was attached, forming the walls. Many of the Babylonian temples used bitumen mixed with the mortar, generally in the proportions 25 to 35% bitumen to 65 to 75% loam and chopped reeds. A Nebuchadnezzar text says, 'Its walls I overlaid with massive gold, as with gypsum and bitumen'. At Mohenjo-Daro in the Indus valley bitumen was used to waterproof a huge tank 39 × 23 ft (11.9 × 7 m), together with its supply and drainage channels, and Herodotus tells us that the walls of Babylon were built of burnt brick cemented by hot bitumen. Bitumen is, of course, familiar to us today as a surfacing material for roads.

Gypsum ($CaSO_4.2H_2O$) has already been mentioned as the mineral of which true alabaster is composed and as one of the possible sources for mortar. It is basically calcium sulphate, but deposits are often contaminated with quartz sand, or with calcium carbonate. It occurs in many different forms, but in hot, arid regions, especially where the bedrock is of limestone, it may be found as irregular nodules just below the surface. Plaster of Paris (hemihydrite plaster) is made by calcining the gypsum at a relatively low temperature, by heating for a few hours thus evaporating some of the water of crystallisation present in the gypsum. In the ancient world this was done using a primitive kiln, fuelled by wood or charcoal. Plaster of Paris sets very rapidly when mixed again with water, and in early times it was often mixed with a little glue (made from animal horns or hoofs cooked in caustic soda) to make building plaster. This varied in colour from white, grey to light brown or even pink, and was sometimes used to cover up irregularities in the stonework. The colour could be deliberately lightened by adding more calcium carbonate, or made a deeper grey by adding a little organic matter derived from unburnt wood. Gypsum is used throughout the world as a building material, and in Britain is obtained by mining the Keuper Marls of Nottinghamshire. It was, however, little used here until the 13th century. Figure 12 shows the uppermost layers of a gypsum bed at McGhie's Quarry, Westmorland. The darker areas are large crystals of selenite.

The production of quicklime from burnt limestone requires a much higher temperature than that necessary for converting

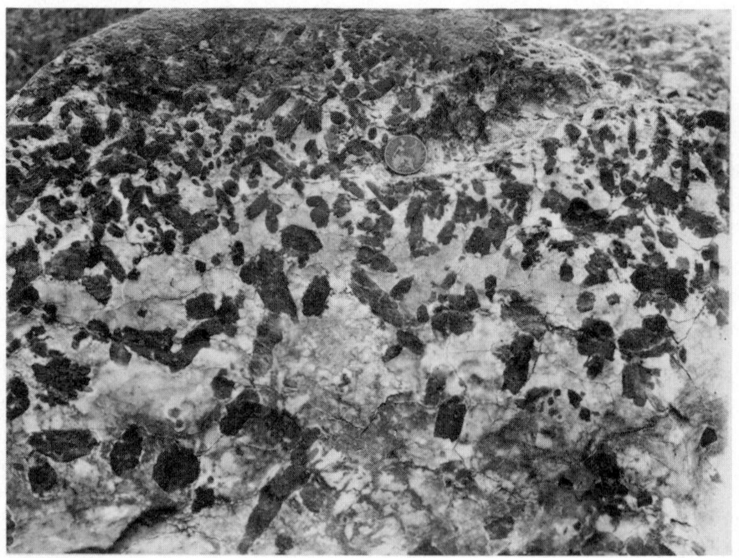

Figure 12. An exposure of gypsum with darker crystals of selenite. Photograph reproduced by kind permission of the Institute of Geological Sciences.

gypsum into Plaster of Paris, and lime burning is everywhere a later development. A cement mortar may be obtained from quicklime by slaking it with water and sand, and in the Roman world a group of materials called 'possolanas' were added which gave the mortar much greater strength. These could be natural products, like volcanic earth or ash, burnt clay, powdered tile, or potsherds. They facilitated the construction of stronger walls, arches and vaults, and the result was water-resistant and therefore suitable for lining baths, drains or aqueducts. After the Roman period there seems to have been a reversal to the use of non-hydraulic mortars, which lasted virtually until the early 19th century, when the industrial revolution required the development of some water-resistant material. The first hydraulic cement used at that time was obtained from nodules of argillaceous limestone from the Tertiary Clays in Kent, but such vast quantities were removed from the coast in the region of Dover and Harwich that a Bill was passed through Parliament stopping the quarrying. The next development was the discovery of Portland cement, where chalk and clay are added and burnt at a sufficiently high temperature to vitrify the material which is then ground to a powder. It seems that the Romans did not discover the Kent source of water-resistant cement, although they built bath blocks of the septarian nodules, bedded in a white lime mortar, little knowing that by burning them a far more durable product would have resulted.

Wall plaster is of very great antiquity, and the art and fashion for plastering walls seems to have started at least as early as the first Neolithic villages of the Near East, as a protective covering for the mudbrick walls as well as a medium for decoration. The use of wall plaster survives, of course, right into the present day, although without the brightly coloured friezes and dados so popular in Neolithic times. Splendid examples of the latter were excavated from Jericho and Çatal Hüyük in Anatolia, and in both cases bright red was a favourite colour. Egyptian wall plaster was similar in composition to their mortar, either a simple clay plaster or a gypsum (lime-based) plaster. Both varieties were probably used for covering the walls of houses, but few fragments have survived, the extant examples coming only from tombs and temples. Clay plaster was often concealed by a coat of the more superior gypsum plaster, especially where the surface was later destined for painting. An exception to this rule is the city of El Amarna, where one of the architecturally revolutionary features seems to have been the use of rough clay plaster without a covering, even as a foundation for the palace murals. This is a reflection of the religious and social climate existing at the time when the city was built, a period of great innovation under the control of the 'heretic' sun-worshipping pharaoh Amenophis IV (Akhenaten), who encouraged a cult of naturalism and simplicity. A certain parallel to this trend can be seen in modern times, where there is a growing movement in favour of rough-textured earthenware pottery, coarse weave curtains, wooden spoons and bowls, thick plain-coloured rugs. Here the ethnic is replacing the stylish, and the trousered piano legs of our grandparents are as foreign to the mood of the moment as the stylised portraiture of his predecessor Amenophis III was to Akhenaten, who defied the time-honoured artistic conventions by having himself reproduced warts and all. This quest for naturalism at the expense of convention revolutionised many features of Egyptian life at the time, but the phase was transient.

The art of fresco consists in applying mineral and earth pigments to lime plaster, requiring considerable skill since the plaster must be at just the right conditions of moisture if the fresco is not to be ruined. Fresco techniques were popular at very early dates, especially in the Minoan civilisation of Crete, and were favoured by the Greeks and Romans. The most outstanding exponent of fresco was undoubtedly Michelangelo, whose painting of the Sistine ceiling in the Vatican occupied four years of his life (1508–1512) and when completed measured 133 × 43 ft (40.5 × 13 m). The fresco painter indicated to the plasterer the area which he intended to cover, and the latter then applied the intonaco, or priming coat. The design was painted onto a slightly damp ground, excess plaster being removed at the end of the day. If the artisans were skilful no join could be seen between work done on different days.

If the gypsum, lime or cement plaster is fashioned into decorative mouldings on the exterior of walls it is referred to as stucco, which was often used in the ancient world as a substitute for dressed and tooled stone. In some countries, such as Iraq, stucco was used as an ornamental covering for brick walls where stone was not plentiful. The walls of the chambers in the pyramids were treated with stucco, and it was also used by the Minoans outside rubble masonry, as a protective covering for walls, as many as four coats being applied. The Romans used stucco mouldings in relief work consisting of at least 50% chalk or lime, the remainder being gravel, sand or crushed tile or clay. Pliny says that stucco never possesses the required brilliance unless three coats of sand mortar were used under two coats of marble stucco (marble, lime and water). Buildings exposed or near the sea needed an undercoat of plaster made from broken potsherds as an additional protection. The architect Pierro Ligorino, who assisted Michelangelo in Rome, has left a fine recipe for the type of stucco used in the Renaissance, the original manuscript being held in the Bodleian library at Oxford.

'Take three parts of pounded Parian marble, easily got from among the ruins in Rome and from broken statues: add one part of lime which is to be prepared by properly slaking by letting it lie in a heap covered with possolana and exposed to the sun and rain for at least a year. The lime is to be made from pure white marble, not from travertine, or any other stone which is full of holes or yellowish in tint. Mix a day before use with sufficient water on a tile floor. The first, or "rendering" coat to be of stucco, made with coarsely pounded marble, allowed to dry throughly before applying the finishing coat of the finely powdered marble cement.'

Stucco was also used in Central America, and beautiful heads were made of this material by the Maya, although the makers were equally accomplished in carving very hard rocks, such as diorite, for statues, friezes and inscriptions.

Tempera colours were also used for wall painting, and were

composed of mixtures of water, pigment and an organic binding substance. The result was then applied to a dry surface, and was sometimes used to cover or 'touch up' frescos. It is a very common technique in Greek, Roman and Egyptian wall painting.

The pigments used for wall painting vary from culture to culture, but certain minerals often recur. Yellow was often obtained from yellow ochre (goethite, $Fe_2O_3.H_2O$), or raw sienna (hydrated ferric oxide with impurities of silica and aluminium). Raw sienna, when burnt, gave a fine red colour, and brown could be obtained from a similar pigment. Red ochre was used from Palaeolithic times onwards, and was mined in Neolithic times in Hungary. It is still used today as a medium for cave painting by the Aborigines, who also obtain it by mining. Black pigments are generally some form of carbon, or charcoal, but blue may be obtained from a wider variety of sources, lapis lazuli for example, which is the source of the valuable ultramarine, and azurite (a basic copper carbonate, $Cu_3(CO_3)_2(OH)_2$). Green may come from malachite (another copper carbonate, $Cu_2CO_3(OH)_2$), or clays rich in glauconite. Purple, dark pink and maroon pigments were usually some form of haematite.

The art of glass manufacture is also of very great antiquity, and is known in Mesopotamia from the 3rd millennium BC. Window glass, however, was not extensively used until Imperial Rome, and even then other materials (alabaster, selenite, mica, horn, parchment) were often substituted. The Byzantine church of San Vitale at Ravenna has windows filled with very thin slabs of marble. Selenite (a crystallised form of gypsum) was sometimes used as a substitute for window glass as late as the 18th century, and the Roman world obtained it from Spain, Cyprus, Cappadocia and Sicily. The Spanish variety was thought to be the best and was dug at great depths by means of shafts. No lumps were found which exceeded 5 ft in length, but it had the great advantage of not seeming to deteriorate in use. True glass is made from silica, as in quartz sand, together with an alkaline base (usually soda, sodium carbonate) or potash (nitre, or saltpetre), mixed with a second alkali such as chalk. All these substances are fused together at temperatures of 1000 to 1300°C, and may be coloured by metal oxides in glazes. Ancient glass sometimes resembled the modern product, with similar constituents but mixed in different proportions. Usually there was more alkali and less silica present, which lowered the firing temperature and made the glass easier to work, but also made it less resistant to damp and other atmospheric conditions which produce decay. The greenish or brownish tints of Medieval glassware are the result of the presence of iron in the sand, but later on it was found that manganese oxide could counteract this effect and produce white glass. Stained glass is of Near Eastern or Byzantine origin, and was fostered in Europe by the Benedictine monks.

Similar pigments are used both for staining glass and to produce coloured glazes for pottery. The basis of a glaze is similar to that of a glass, containing silica, an alkali and often some chalk, which is then mixed to a paste with water, applied to the clay body, and fired. If the clay is not highly siliceous the mixture will not adhere well, but this can be improved by the addition of lead, which has the additional advantage of lowering the required firing temperature. The earliest recipe for glaze comes from a Babylonian text, dated to 1700 BC, written on a clay tablet. It mentions the ingredients potash, lime, copper and lead, and a similar, but later text, found on an Assyrian tablet from the Royal Library at Ninevah (which was set up by Assur-bani-pal 668–634 BC) describes the addition of another alkali, antimony and arsenic to glazes. The lead content of a glaze is added as lead oxide (lithage or red lead), lead carbonate (white lead), or lead sulphide (galena). Metal oxides usually make the colouring materials for glazes, iron giving green, or red, cobalt to give blue, manganese and nickel oxides for purple, brown and maroon. Cupric oxide under strong reducing conditions gives a red glaze, chromium oxide a yellowish grey and tin oxides give white. White glazes can also be obtained by adding bone ash (calcium phosphate), fluorspar or cryolite. More exotic colorants include selenium for a brilliant red and the rich ruby colour which is obtained from finely divided gold.

CHAPTER 4

Building stone

'Under this stone, Reader, survey
Dead Sir John Vanburgh's house of clay.
Lie heavy on him, Earth! for he
Laid many heavy loads on thee!'

(Abel Evans, 1679–1737, Epitaph on Sir John Vanburgh, Architect of Blenheim Palace)

Human priorities seem to have remained virtually fixed since the earliest times, namely food, clothing and shelter, in that order. Indeed the need to obtain these better and more efficiently than one's neighbours has been the chief motivating force in history. Crude wind-breaks were made by the first hominids, simple shelters consisting of a pile of stones, or a skin weighed down at the bottom with bones or rocks. The remains of such foundations have been excavated at Olduvai (p. 45), associated with pebble-tool cultures, and other examples of the weights for tent-stances have been found on Middle Palaeolithic sites in France and Russia. Early man also made use of caves and rock shelters, frequently modifying and adapting them by the addition of wooden structures, the narrowing of entrances and the construction of internal walls. The first stone-built houses appear in early proto-Neolithic times in the Near East but usually stone construction was used for public buildings, tombs, temples and monuments, rather than for domestic architecture. Such building works imply great control over manpower resources, as well as a technology sufficiently advanced to design and supervise the quarrying, moving, erection and finishing of the stones.

The type of stone used in building clearly varies from culture to culture, depending on local availability, and technological skills. In early times sedimentary rocks were chosen, because they are easier to work than igneous or metamorphic facies. Fossiliferous building stones may often be assigned to their geological age, and thus to a source area within the limits of outcropping. The finding of stones outside this area implies transport, although the possibility that minor outliers have remained undetected must always be kept in mind. Much of the work of identification is palaeontological, on the basis of both macro- and microfossils of plants and animals, although 'heavy' mineral suites and the inclusion of particles such as glauconite (a hydrated silicate of iron and potassium) may be helpful. Microfossils (ostracods, foraminifera, sponge spicules etc.) are often widely and uniformly dispersed through a rock, and are very helpful where the sample is of a limited size, especially with the best freestones whose very quality lies in their freedom from the larger fossils. The character of sedimentary rocks reflects the condition of their deposition and any subsequent deformation, and it must always be remembered that lithologically similar rocks may be found widely separated in time and place.

The Egyptians were the earliest people to make extensive use of stone for building, principally limestones and sandstones, with lesser quantities of granite and occasional use of basalt, alabaster and quartzite. The main building limestone outcrops for a distance of 500 miles in the hills bordering the Nile Valley, as well as in numerous other localities. It was generally quarried very near where it was required, except for the better quality stones which were obtained from permanent quarries, including those at Tura, Masara, Ayan and Gebelein, where period inscriptions can still be seen today on the quarry walls. Cairo museum contains a letter (no. 49623) written on papyrus by an officer in charge of certain Tura quarrymen in the 6th Dynasty (3rd millennium BC), and the same quarry is still being worked today. Basalt, a black, heavy compact fine-grained igneous rock, was used in the Old Kingdom (2686–2181 BC) for pavements, as well as in building. Quartzite, a hard white or yellow metamorphosed sandstone, also had a specialised use for the thresholds of doorways or as a lining for chambers. Granite was also employed from the Dynastic period onwards as a lining material for chambers, together with passages and door frames. The favourite variety was the coarse-grained red granite from Aswan, but a dark grey hornblende-biotite granite was quarried from the same source area. The principal Egyptian granite quarries were always those of Aswan, but in Roman times use was made of the black and white granite quarried from Mons Claudianum in the Eastern desert.

Contemporary classical literature on building stone is very meagre, except for the work of Vitruvius (*De Architectura*) and the comments of Pliny. Much more information can be obtained from a study of the buildings which survive, Romano-British stone sources especially having been the focus of much attention, to see whether they can throw any light on the economic history of the period. Clearly the type of building stone used influences architectural styles, and is itself conditioned by the available stone sources and the distance which the builders were prepared to trade. Other determining factors would include the type of building and, perhaps the most important, the wealth of the builder. The vast resources commanded by the builders of a palace such as Fishbourne would not have been at the disposal of even the wealthiest of private individuals, and it seems probable that it was largely financed by the government. Fishbourne is located near Chichester in Sussex, and was excavated between 1961 and 1969; the site and extant mosaics now being the focus of a museum. Use was made of local stones, such as the fine grained glauconitic sandstone from the Church Rocks reef at West Wittering, and a silty limestone with mica flakes from Pulborough, Sussex. The first period 'proto-palace' (Neronian to early Flavian in date, *c.* AD 70) used six different building stones, including two nummulitic limestones from the Mediterranean, and blocks of igneous stone from the west coasts of Britain and France incorporated into the wall fittings. Hornblende diorites were

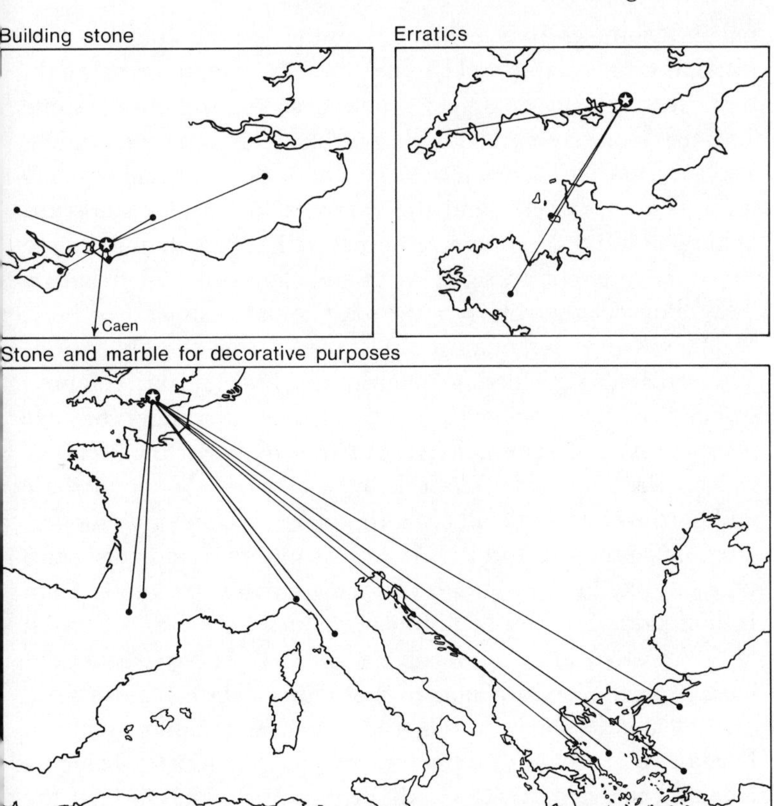

Figure 13. Sources of stone for the Flavian Palace at Fishbourne, Sussex, showing the great diversity of types used and the distances from which material was imported.

imported, probably from Jersey, epidiorite from Cornwall and schists from Brittany. All the remnants of these hard rocks showed signs of water wear, and it is thought that they were brought as ballast in ships using the harbour during the early years of the Roman occupation. Figure 13 illustrates the great diversity of the stone sources. Even more varieties of stone were used in the later, more spectacular, Flavian palace, varying from local calcites (as an ingredient in wall plaster), glauconitic sandstones from the Weald for gutter blocks, and Mediterranean white limestones and Caen stone from France for the palace columns. It is evident that the masons had at their disposal large quantities of stone carefully chosen for its qualities, expense being no object. Numerous other varieties of stone and marble were used for decorative inlay work, including Purbeck 'marble', French breccias and sandstones and marbles from Turkey, Greece, and the Pyrenees. A mason's workyard belonging to the Neronian proto-palace has been found, where the stone was cut to serve as mouldings, wall and furniture inlay. Purbeck 'marble' was the most common stone used here, together with lesser quantities of breccia from the Cote d'Or. The yard also yielded geometric elements of the coloured stones used in *opus sectile* pavements, a forerunner of true mosaic. Five different rocks were used; red and yellow Mediterranean siltstone, blue Purbeck 'marble', grey Wealden shale and hard white Chalk, all cut into squares, triangles, diamonds, kites, octagons and strips. It is a great pity that no floor of this type survives from Fishbourne, although many are known from Italian sites. Marbles of different colours were also employed for decorative inlay in furniture, as well as for basins and tesserae in the mosaic floors of the second palace (AD 75–80).

Flint and Chalk were sometimes used as building stones in Roman Britain, the latter, surprisingly enough, being a favoured lining material for the hypocausts which formed the Roman underfloor central heating system. Flint nodules embedded in mortar were used for walls, the strength of which was largely determined by the quality of the mortar. Flint walls were also often strengthened by the inclusion of bonding courses, horizontally laid tiles and flat stones, which can be seen in stretches of the walls of towns and late coastal forts such as Portchester Castle, Hampshire (Fig. 14). Greensand, a much harder stone than Chalk, is easy to work and fairly durable, and was extensively used both for building and as a raw material for quernstones. It was in use in London before the Boudiccan revolt of AD 60, and continued to be fashionable right through the Roman period. Tufa was popular because of its lightness, and is sometimes to be found in the remains of bath houses. The Purbeck 'marble' from the Upper Jurassic beds of the Isle of Purbeck has been already mentioned, and

Figure 14. Tile courses in a bastion of the Roman wall, Portchester Castle, Hampshire.

was also a building material very popular with English Medieval architects for sepulchral monuments and columns. It consists of shells of the fresh water gastropod *Paludina caranifera*, embedded in greenish or bluish-grey limestone, producing a very attractive stone. Such decorative stones were not widely traded, but used intensively in the general area where they occurred; for example the orange, shelly Ham Hill stone from the Upper Lias near Ilchester, or the Ketton stone, which was transported via the Car Dyke to Verulamium from its source in Lincolnshire. Most public buildings incorporated many different types of stone, few using only local materials, but none reached the proliferation of different stone types employed at Fishbourne. The Romans seem, however, to have been especially fond of marble (metamorphosed limestone), and to have been willing to transport favourite varieties for very long distances. At Colchester the marbles used included a green and white banded type from quarries on the Greek island of Euboea, a white crystalline marble from Italy, a yellow marble with red veins from Algeria, and many other types. The same site produced some green porphyry from quarries near Sparta, all these exotics having been transported a thousand miles or so by land and sea, to a town then situated at the extreme fringe of the Roman Empire.

Greek architects also used marbles, but they preferred white or light-coloured stones, especially the close-grained Pentelic variety from Attica, the translucent marbles of Paros and Naxos and soft-coloured stones from the Greek mainland. Very little use was made of multi-coloured stones until Roman times, although they were available. The Roman passion for rather florid stones was passed on in due course to Byzantium, where coloured marbles and ornamental stones were often combined in the very worst of taste, the resulting buildings making up in magnificence for what they lacked in aesthetic appeal.

The quarrying and mining of building stone has a very long history. In England the earliest mines were of Neolithic date, sunk in the Chalk of East Anglia and the Marlborough Downs for flint as raw material for tools, not as building stone. It was not until the coming of the Romans that any large-scale quarrying operations were initiated, although some small quarries must have been operating before that date to supply the raw materials for whetstones, axes and querns. Stone quarries were established remarkably quickly after the conquest, wherever suitable rock could be found. The early growth of such industries, which require technical knowledge, suggests exploitation by masons from abroad. The same might be said of the early flourishing of tile-making and pottery production, enterprises stimulated by immigrant speculators and the new trading opportunities with Continental merchants. There was gradually increasing production of good building stone during the 2nd and subsequent centuries, as town buildings ceased to be half-timbered, and demand was increased by the erection of private and public monuments, town walls and villas. Some of the quarries still specialised in material for domestic millstones, and in the south these tended to be made from Greensand or the conglomerate called Hertfordshire Puddingstone, composed of black- to brown-skinned flint pebbles embedded in a matrix of fine quartzitic sandstone indistinguishable from sarsen-stone. Millstone Grit was used in the Pennines, and a workshop for this material has been found at Wharncliff Rocks, near Sheffield. A quarry specifically for whetstones was operating near Stony Stratford, and its products were clearly distributed by road and are found as far away as London, Wroxeter and Richborough.

Classical quarrying operations were sometimes carried out on a vast scale, as in Sicily where the great limestone quarries of Syracuse have a face 90 ft (27 m) high and 1¼ miles (2 km) long, together with galleries driven deep into the rock. It was estimated that over forty million cubic tons of stone had been extracted, and the size of the operation can be further illustrated by the fact that 7 000 Athenian prisoners were employed there in 413 BC after the defeat of Athens by Sparta.

Picks, bars and wedges are still used for quarrying sedimentary rocks, advantage being taken of the natural bedding planes. Figure 15 shows that quarrying techniques do indeed vary only slightly with time! To utilise the stone to its best advantage from the point of view of strength and resistance to weathering it is customary nowadays to lay it on its natural bedding plane, if it has one, or in such a way that the bedding plane is at right angles to the thrust. Thus the stones for an arch are cut and placed so that their natural bedding planes lie radially, a technique that was also used in the ancient world. The Egyptian method of quarrying sedimentary rocks has been described by many authors, and is based on the simple principle that wood expands when moistened. In order to detach a block of stone grooves were cut along four sides, wooden wedges driven in, and then saturated with water to make them swell. This cracked the seams and the block could be prised up with wooden levers. This method was, however, only suitable for sedimentary rocks with well-defined bedding

Figure 15. Quarrying techniques for sandstone, Ham Hill quarry. Photograph reproduced by kind permission of the Institute of Geological Sciences.

planes, the harder igneous or metamorphic rocks presenting much more serious problems. It seems likely that in later Egyptian times the harder rocks were quarried by hammering with rock balls and that slots were then cut with a metal tool, wooden wedges again being driven in to complete the process. This procedure and the finished blocks are portrayed in tomb paintings, for example the 18th-Dynasty tomb of Rekhmare at Thebes. Here a granite statue is shown being finished off by pounding with stones, and large blocks of limestone being squared off by chiselling. Cutting may have been helped by an abrasive such as emery, fed to a soft metal blade, and drilling facilitated by feeding this abrasive down a soft copper tube, a technique that is still used today for boring holes in glass. Softer stones, like limestone, could be cut and finished with a toothed saw. Such limestone would have either been obtained from surface quarrying, as at Giza, or by tunnelling, as at Tura. The finest limestone, as with the richest veins of minerals, is generally to be found well below the surface. In the tunnel quarry a deep shelf-like hollow extending across the breadth of the passage was cut between the roof and the first block to be detached, enabling the quarrymen to crawl across the top of the rock and work its farther edge, chipping downwards with a chisel struck by a wooden mallet. Tunnelling was never adopted for rocks such as granite, although the wedge-removal method was used, the marks of the wedge-slots still being visible today in the granite quarries at Aswan. It has been suggested that the slots were made either by rubbing an abrasive powder into the stone, or else by the use of a metal tool. If metal was used it must have been copper, which is very soft, since the art of alloying with lead or tin to give the harder product, bronze, had not yet been discovered. It is possible that some process was being used which would give a very high temper to copper tools, since they would have been useless on very hard rocks such as granite. The alternative method of detaching the blocks by pounding with dolerite balls is the more likely. Dolerite is found over a wide area of the eastern desert near the Red Sea. An unfinished New Kingdom (1567–1085 BC) obelisk, still lying in the quarry at Aswan, was undoubtedly worked by this method. It is also probable that the workers exploited the use of fire, alternately heating the rock and then cooling it with cold water to encourage selective disintegration and then crumbling. The dolerite balls used for pounding weighed about 10 lb (4.5 kg) apiece, and an experiment on the Aswan granite showed that a skilled mason using them to pound the rock for 1 hour reduced its level by around 5 mm within his work area. From this it was calculated that the Aswan obelisk would have required at least 15 months' work by a team of 400 men, an upper team of 260 men ramming dolerite balls at the granite, and a further 140 men in trenches clearing away the dust. The stones used in the construction of the sarsen trilithons at Stonehenge are at least twice as hard as granite. The available tools must have been similar but the workforce less well organised, and undoubtedly less practised. It was calculated that 50 masons working 10 hours a day all the year round would have taken 3 years to dress the stones by grinding and pounding, and extra time would have been needed for the fashioning of the mortice and tenon joints for linking uprights to capstones. The sheer size of the undertaking is often underestimated. Granite, basalt and sarsen will blunt good modern steel tools very quickly. Nineteenth-century French workmen, using the best tools available to them, took six weeks to cut a small groove around the base of an obelisk at Luxor before removing it from its pedestal.

The Aztecs also worked stone without the use of metal tools, by flaking and chipping for the hard stones, pecking and hammering for the softer ones, both procedures requiring great patience and skill. Final polish was obtained from a simple water-and-sand mixture. Some harder stones were detached from their matrix by applying the abrasive and sawing with a piece of rawhide, or with some harder stone. Instead of the copper tubes used in Egypt the Aztecs used tubular drills of bone or reed, rotated by a bow and aided by an abrasive. This technique was utilised especially for hollowing-out vases, and for boring complex designs.

In Roman times saws without teeth were used for hard stone, also in company with an abrasive, the toothed saws being reserved for softer material. Later the saws were driven by water power and were able to cut very large blocks comparatively quickly, such as the 36 ft (11 m) diameter roof stone for the cupola of the tomb of Theodoric at Ravenna, built in AD 530. The Romans were also highly skilled in the finishing of stone for masonry purposes, as at Fishbourne, where the surviving fragments of columns, each section weighing over half a ton, show signs of having been dressed by turning on a lathe. At the same site blocks of hard Italian Carrara marble are found, from which very thin sheets have been removed for wall inlay. These Carrara marble quarries were first worked in 100 BC, and are described by Strabo. An 80-ton block of this marble was used in Trajan's column, and the quarries were still being exploited in Medieval and Renaissance times, the finest sculptures of Michelangelo being executed in this marble. Pliny says, 'The art of cutting marble into thin slabs (veneer) may possibly have been invented in Caria (where there is a famous source of white first-quality marble). The earliest instance, so far as I can discover, is that of the palace of

Mausolus at Halicarnassus, the brick walls of which were decorated with marble from the islands of Marmara' (*Natural History*, 36.46).

This building, the Mausoleum, was built in 353 BC, and is counted as one of the 'Seven Wonders of the World'. The veneer slabs were obtained by sawing with toothless blades and sand pressed into a thinly traced line. Roman masons preferred Ethiopian sand, since it was supposed to cut without leaving roughness, Indian sand being the next choice. The coarser the sand used the less accurate the sections.

All the ways used in antiquity for moving stones require a large labour force, and refinements such as rollers, sledges, or wooden cribs are incidental to the manpower. The most impressive surviving examples of large-scale stone moving are surely to be found in Egypt, in the Pyramids whose combined weights of millions of tons represent untold man-hours of quarrying, moving, fitting and finishing. Neither written nor pictorial records throw any light on the method of construction of these vast monuments, but this has been deduced from a close study of the buildings themselves, and of the tools known to have been available at the time. The stones were moved from the quarry to the site principally by water, using no sophisticated equipment, the stone foundations of the Pyramid causeway always being laid first so that they could be used for the later passage of material up to the pyramid itself. The transport of the great blocks remains a remarkable engineering feat. The casing blocks for the Great Pyramid average 2½ tons in weight, and the roof slabs of the King's Chamber 50 tons each. Even these pale before the heaviest pieces from the mortuary temple of Mycerinus, estimated by Reisner to weigh 500 tons each. The difficulties of moving such blocks should not be under-estimated. A very large and well-disciplined work force was required, and if the blocks were moved during the annual Nile flood this could, of course, have been utilised. The lands of the peasant farmers would have been under water and they were no doubt glad to, or at any rate obliged to, work for the wages which Pharaoh offered. Slave labour does not seem to have been involved, and there are letters still in existence that testify to the wages paid, which seem partly to have been in kind (clothes, food etc.). It seems from paintings that sledges and rollers were used to move the heaviest blocks, the power being supplied by gangs of men. A ratio of about 3 men per ton of statue has been calculated from an illustration showing a statue in the actual process of being transported from the tomb of Djerhuihotep, a 12th Dynasty (1991–1786 BC) nobleman buried at El Bershesh. Water was probably poured on the ground to lessen the friction and help the haulage, and it seems likely that the work proceeded along fixed rhythms beaten out regularly from some form of musical instrument.

Herodotus says that the Great Pyramid was built in tiers, battlement-wise, the upper part being finished first. Since the pulley does not seem to have been known in pre-Roman Egypt the only suitable method of construction was to build a series of sloping brick and earth ramps from ground level to the required height. With the addition of each course of masonry the ramp would be raised and extended so that its gradient remained unchanged. After the wall in question had been finished the ramp would be dismantled, and the outer casings dressed course by course downwards as the dismantling proceeded. An example of such a ramp could be seen until recent times against the unfinished First Pylon of the temple at Karnak. The gradient of the ramp probably depended upon the weight of the material to be conveyed, varying between 1 in 8 and 1 in 12. It has been suggested that a single supply ramp was made to cover the whole of one side of a pyramid, and as the pyramid rose in height the ramp increased in both height and length, the top becoming progressively narrower to correspond with the decreasing breadth of the pyramid face. After the core of the structure had been completed the facing blocks were then added, a more delicate undertaking since an error in the placing of a single block would throw out the whole symmetry of the structure. It seems likely that the fitting of the joints between neighbouring blocks of the same course was carried out at ground level by highly skilled masons. This would have left only the final dressing to be done when the block was nearly in place, and it remained only to move the block into position with its film of mortar acting as a lubricant. The mean opening of the joints of the casing blocks of the Great Pyramid was estimated by Petrie to be .01 in (.25 mm). It is possible that some of the capstones were overlaid with gold, and certainly evidence suggests that they were sometimes elaborately carved. The corridors and chambers of the interior of the pyramid were finished before the core structure, and fittings such as the portcullis and sarcophagus positioned before the walls of the chambers or galleries had been built.

Heyerdahl, in his investigations of the giant statues and culture of Easter Island in the Pacific, provided a graphic illustration of the comparative ease with which skilled men could move large pieces of masonry. In an experimental raising of a giant statue, one side was lifted 30 ft (9 m) into the air on a gradually growing heap of stones. The process took only about a dozen men and occupied 18 days, the only tools being poles and ropes. On the last day the final trick was to hold the statue by the ropes and prevent it toppling off the high wall, while it was finally hauled into a standing position.

The same principle, replacing sophisticated engineering by manpower and very simple tools, was used in many other prehistoric stone-moving operations, for example in the construction of Stonehenge. Many of the earliest monuments were built with stone deliberately chosen for particular properties, often requiring transport from some distance away. The bluestone circle of Stonehenge (II) is a case in point, built from various stones probably imported from the Prescelly mountains in South Wales. These stones must have travelled at least 150 miles (240 km) by a circuitous route to their final resting place on Salisbury Plain. Richard Atkinson describes an experiment in which a replica of one of the bluestones, weighing just under 2 tons, was made and transported up the River Avon to near Stonehenge. It was found that the stone could quite easily be moved on a raft propelled by two schoolboys with poles, and that such a simple craft would easily navigate shallow rivers and creeks. Clearly a large reserve of manpower was not required for that stage in the process, but it would certainly have been needed for the final treck overland, and indeed for the initial quarrying and final erection of the stones. The bluestone replica could be moved quite easily by a team of 12 men, pulling it along on a sledge, a further 12 being required to collect and replace the rollers. This is by far and away the easiest method of transporting large stones, but it would have been possible to move the blocks, just by dragging on wooden sledges, although this would have presented problems of friction and also required more labour. In this experiment $2\frac{1}{2}$ times more men were required to move the stone by dragging than were needed for transport involving rollers, giving a figure of 16 men per ton of stone. On this basis at least 100 men would have been required to drag the largest of the bluestones. The huge sarsens of the trilithons, weighing 25 tons each, would have needed huge sledges and would have been much easier to move using rollers. They came from the Marlborough Downs, a distance of at least 20 miles (32 km), and would have needed 880 men each, moving the stone at about 1100 yds (1 km) per day. This means that the entire sarsen complement of stones would have occupied 1500 men full time for 5 years, just to move the stones, and even more men to finish and dress them. The final erection of the sarsens was carried out with the help of a strategically dug pit, a pair of shearlegs and some rope. Some interesting experiments were carried out using scale models of the original stones, which are up to $29\frac{1}{2}$ ft (9 m) tall, at a scale of 1/12. A hole was dug to receive the base of the stone,

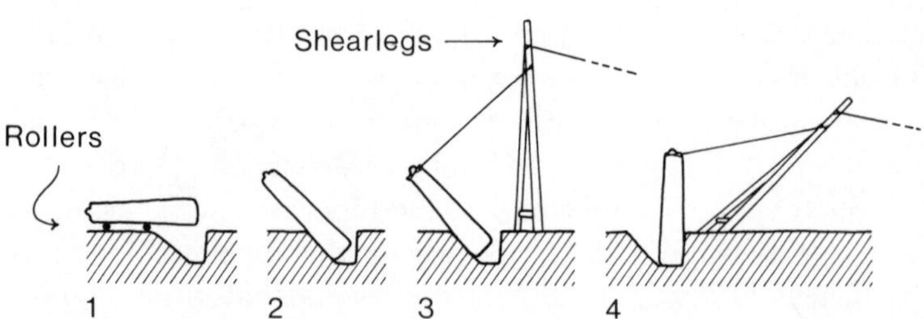

Figure 16. Method of erecting one of the sarsens of Stonehenge, Wiltshire, after Coles (1973): (1) pit dug to receive the stone; (2) stone rolled so that it rested on the 45° sloping bank; (3)–(4) raising of the stone by means of shearlegs and rope, the final hole being packed with pebbles.

with a sloping ramp (Fig. 16) at an angle of 45° facing the stone, and a vertical face opposite. The stone, placed on rollers, was pushed gently forward until it overlapped the hole, and tipped in so that it rested on the 45° axis ramp. A pair of shear-legs were positioned on the opposite side of the hole and a crossbar lashed to the top of the stone. Ropes joined this to the shearlegs so that the pull of the rope was at right angles to the plane of the stone. The shearlegs were raised by hauling on ropes attached to the top, and gradually the stone was lifted into a vertical position, the hole being tightly packed with stones. At least 180 men would be needed to raise one of the 26 ton sarsens into position, and the positioning of the lintels on top of the capstones was an even more complicated matter. Each lintel is carved with a tongue at one and and a groove at the other to fit its neighbouring stones in the circle, and each has two mortice holes on one broad face which were to be positioned over the two tenons of each of the uprights. Three different methods for lifting and positioning the lintels have been proposed. One involves the building of a large earthen bank around each upright, with a gently inclined ramp leading up to the top. The idea is that the lintel could have been moved up the ramp by ropes tied twice around it and then fastened to bollard posts, with an arrangement of pulleys, ropes, rollers and bearers turning the lintel over and over up the ramp, a manoeuvre requiring about 150 men. The ramp theory is, of course, based on the ramps postulated for the construction of the pyramids. The second theory involves the construction of a timber ramp instead of an earthen one, which would dispose of the objection that there is no sign of a quarry for material to build an earthen ramp. Unfortunately the post holes for such a timber ramp do not seem to have existed either. The last method, involving the use of a timber crib, would have been the easiest to make and dismantle, consisting of a series of wooden beams and planks levered gradually upwards in a manner similar to that seen in the raising of the Easter Island statues. Only about 75 men would have been needed, and very little timber.

All these experiments lead one to conclude that only the

simplest tools were required even for moving extremely large lumps of stone. The important thing is not the sophistication of the machinery but the degree of motivation and the organisation of the workforces.

Megalithic tombs have also been the subject of much interest and speculation amongst antiquaries and, later, amongst archaeologists. In the old days interest was focused on such matters as the size and weight of the capstones, but later in time more systematic studies concentrated on plans, using them as a guide to cultural connections and even to relative chronological positions. Factors of building technique were clearly involved in the choice of location, and as far as tombs on slopes and hollows were concerned questions of economy in the transport and lifting of the heavy slabs arose. The fact that so many tombs were built on hill tops and crests surely represents the triumph of ritual over economic motives. The source material everywhere is local stone. Megalithic tombs are not, however, always found in places where suitable rocks occur, but suitable sources of stone for the heavy slabs are found within a few hundred yards of most tombs. The structural character of available rocks must have affected the scale and appearance of tombs but, as Henshall points out, building stone is found only to influence, not to determine the architectural concept. Stone was imported for special purposes, for example oolite brought over 20 miles for the walling at West Kennett long barrow near Avebury, Wiltshire. Timber slipways were probably used for moving the heavy slabs, similar to those laid down by Neolithic peoples across the peat of the Somerset levels. Elevation of such slabs was done by leverage and building up from underneath the slab to be moved, sliding it onto the intended uprights after the correct height had been reached. Corcoran comments, ‘It is reasonable to suggest that the construction of stone built cairns was influenced by, and possibly derived from, that of earthen long barrows, whatever may have been the origin of the latter’. The floruit of both types seems to have been broadly contemporary. On ceasing to be used for burial both chambered cairns and earthen long barrows were

Figure 17. Blocking wall, West Kennet megalithic tomb, Wiltshire.

Figure 18. Architectural devices: (1) the principle of corbelling, (2) Relieving triangle to take the weight off the lintel of the Lion Gate, Mycenae, Greece.

carefully sealed. In the former this often consisted of a stone blocking wall sealing the chamber entrance (Fig. 17) and in the latter the mound was raised to cover structures such as burial platforms and mortuary enclosures which had hitherto served as foci of funerary ritual.

Some megalithic tombs employ the architectural device known as corbelling, which was widely used in the ancient world for roofing over large spaces. It consists of building a masonry pile with each stone projecting out into the centre of the space (Fig. 18) a little further than the one below. The overhang can be narrowed, if desired, to form a dome. A fine example of this occurs in the 'Treasury of Atreus' in Mycenae, where the corbelled vault exceeds 45 ft (13.7 m) in diameter. The principle is also seen in the megalithic tombs of Spain, and in the corbelled vault of the sanctuary in the temple of Seti I in Egypt. The Mycenean tomb was constructed by driving a roofless horizontal passage into the hillside, to meet a cylindrical shaft dug down from above. A circular chamber was then constructed within the shaft, the walls built in by corbelling to form a pointed dome, the apex of which protruded above ground level and was then covered with a mound. The open sides of the entrance passage of this and other *tholos* tombs were liable to collapse and were therefore lined with masonry, and layers of waterproof clay introduced into the covering mould to prevent seepages which would weaken the dome. The massive lintel stone of the doorway has to have the pressure relieved by the construction of an open corbelled triangle above it, or else even the massive stone would have shattered from the great weight of the vault. The same device is used in the Lion Gate of Mycenae, which has a corbelled relieving triangle over the lintel, and in the corbell-vaulted megalithic tomb of New Grange in Ireland. The principle of the relieving triangle is a very well known architectural device, and was also employed in the construction of the pyramids.

The so called 'Cyclopean' walls of the Greek Bronze Age are probably the most impressive megalithic contructions seen in Europe. They are made of huge irregular pieces of stone, often weighing several tons, and only roughly trimmed. The name comes from the later belief that such walls were too immense to have been man-made, and that they must be the work of the race of Thracian giants called Cyclops. The interstices of the huge blocks were filled with smaller pieces of stone, sometimes bedded in clay, but this form was soon replaced by wall construction using polygonal blocks cut with straight or nearly straight facets. Examples of Cyclopean masonry may also be found in Asia Minor and in the Middle East, and there are some very imposing Persian constructions in the Bakhtiani mountains. The earliest Cyclopean walls tend everywhere to be crude, but later the surfaces of the exposed stones were smoothed, and the angles shaped so that there was no need to fill the crevices with smaller blocks. Polygonal stone walling is the next logical step, seen to perfection in the elegant walls of Inca cities such as Manchu Piccu in Peru (Fig. 19).

The 'wheelhouses' of the Bronze/Iron Age settlement of Jarlshof in Shetland are examples of another stone construction technique, arising from the difficulty of roofing over large buildings. A series of internal radial walls had to be introduced, dividing the area into smaller elements which could then be roofed by corbelling. Still in the Outer Hebrides the Neolithic village of Skara Brae shows another method of house construction, in an area where no large supplies of wood were to be found, and the houses had perforce to be made of stone. They were made from the local flagstone, and were rectangular in plan with rounded corners, partially roofed by corbelling. The finishing slabs for the top of the roof seem likely to have been whalebone. Each house was entered by a low doorway and the furniture, two-tiered dressers of stone slabs, bed-enclosures, sunken recesses and boxes, was all fabricated out of the same stone.

Architectural styles can also be used as a dating technique, especially in the case of churches. In Saxon England churches were virtually the only buildings made of stone, royal domestic buildings even of palatial scale being built entirely of timber, as illustrated by the recent excavations at Yeavering. Church building must have made great demands on contemporary organisation, bulk transport and technological resources. Few

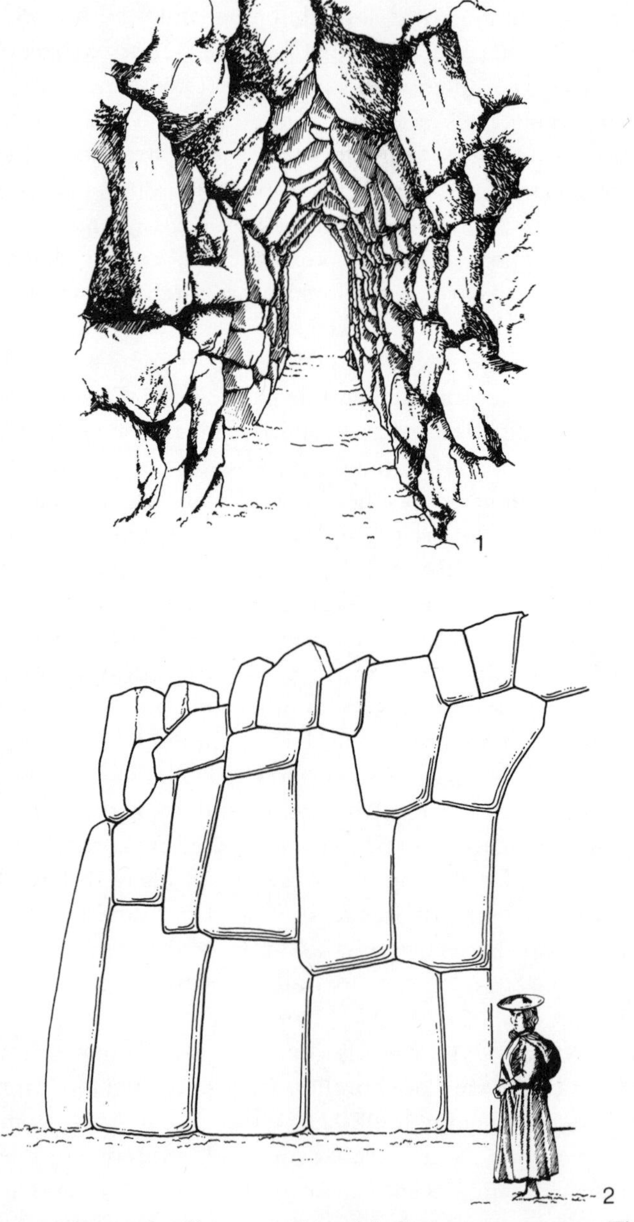

Figure 19. Types of wall construction: (1) Cyclopean masonry, Tiryns, Greece, (2) Polygonal masonry, Inca walls of Manchu Pichu, Peru.

documentary sources are available for a study of Saxon building, and as with most studies of this kind the evidence must be obtained from the buildings themselves.

Building a stone church was a highly organised operation, involving many different craftsmen, carpenters as well as masons and contemporary heavy industrial lifting gear. Only the very wealthy could instigate the building of a church, and many were erected on royal lands or by wealthy laymen, as well as those sponsored by the great monastic houses. There is a widespread uniformity in the use of particular kinds of stone for specific architectural purposes, which indicates a body of transmitted technique and some degree of co-operation among the masons, at least in southern England. Jope suggests that this was based on their contacts at the quarries, many of which were themselves under royal or monastic ownership. The larger monastic establishments, such as Glastonbury, had their own works departments.

A characteristic feature of Saxon church architecture is the double window, with a mid-wall shaft supporting a through stone slab. Doorways and windows are typically triangular headed, and long-and-short quoins are very common, where the angles of the buildings have been constructed by laying large stones in such a way that tall upright pillar stones alternate with broad flat stones that serve to bond the uprights firmly into the wall (Fig. 20). The Normans also used double windows, but of quite a different type. The church of St Mary at Deerhurst (Tewkesbury, Gloucestershire) possesses many typically Anglo-Saxon features, including floors, windows and a font of differing architectural styles. The fabric of the church is of rough coarse rubble, with areas of herringbone work, another feature typical of the period. Figure 20 shows an example of this fabric, achieved by laying thin stones in diagonal course to produce a wall of courses of constant height, even if the stones were of varying thickness. If the courses are laid alternately in opposite directions a decorative pattern is produced. This feature is not, however, solely confined to Anglo-Saxon churches, but it is unquestionably more common there than in Norman or later masonry.

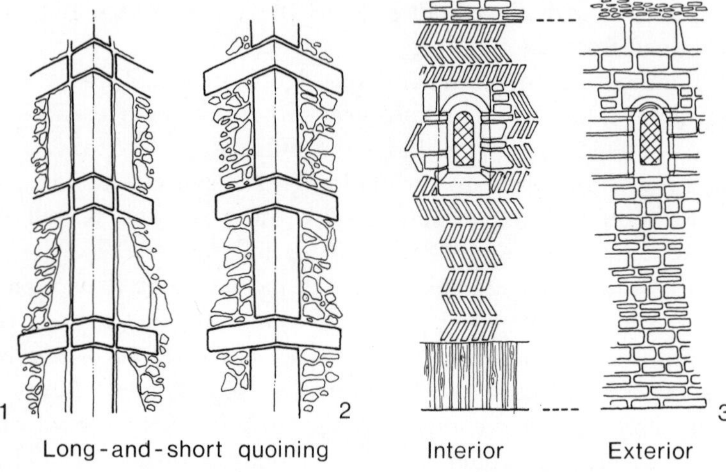

Figure 20. Saxon architectural features: (1) and (2) long-and-short quoins. In (1) the upright pillar stones at the corner of the wall are random in shape, and in (2) the stones are set flush with the main face of the wall. (3) Herringbone masonry in a section of the north wall of the nave, Diddlebury church, Shropshire. (4) Anglo-Saxon type of double arched window. After Davey (1961).

For the dating of the post-Conquest churches the evidence is firmly established in written records, enabling large numbers of buildings to be precisely dated since the features which survive can be identified in detail with features recorded as having been built at specific dates, and sometimes even by specific persons. There is a great lack of similar historical evidence for Anglo-Saxon churches, with the sole exception of St Augustine's Abbey at Canterbury. Different methods must therefore be used, and for dating such buildings the study of the actual construction methods employed comes into its own.

CHAPTER 5

Cosmetics, jewellery and ornaments

'*Why so large cost, having so short a lease,*
Dost thou upon thy fading mansion spend?'

(Shakespeare. Sonnet 146)

Cosmetics are as old as vanity. The use of perfumes and cosmetics is an almost universal practice, except where there is some form of religious or social taboo, as, for example, in 17th-century Puritan England. This does not mean, however, that in a society which does make some use of cosmetics they are necessarily worn by everybody, and often they are restricted to the more leisured (and wealthy) classes. In the present day cosmetics are used as beauty aids almost solely by women, but this has not always been the case. Even now there is a growing tendency for 'respectable' young men to wear some form of cosmetic, and male use of perfumes is becoming widespread, disguised as 'after shave' and marketed under virile names to counteract the lingering feeling that their use is both effete and effeminate. So strong is the pull of vanity that a woman will use a 'beauty' aid even when its constituents are known to be harmful. Hand-whitening lotions containing arsenic were still common in Victorian times, together with face-paints made from various red and white salts of lead. The latter cause horrifying boils and ulcers but their use was very widespread until quite recently. The problem is far from being a modern one, and Ovid says:

> '*Dicebam medicare tuos desiste capillos,*
> *tingere quam possis iam tibi nulla coma est*'
> (Amores XIV 1–28)

('I told you to stop using that rinse, and now you've no hair left to tint')

Graves containing traces of haematite (often called red ochre) are found dating back as far as Palaeolithic times. Red ochre (iron ore, Fe_2O_3), which was principally used as a painting medium, seems to have formed an essential feature of the burial ritual, probably functioning as a blood-symbol. It was later used extensively as a cosmetic. Many kinds of such red pigments are commonly found in Egyptian graves, and they occur at even earlier dates at Çatal Hüyük, sometimes in association with obsidian mirrors. It has generally been assumed that they were used as some form of rouge, although this very reasonable hypothesis is as yet unsupported by any form of documentary or archaeological evidence. The pigments are often associated with the palettes or stones on which they were ground, and one example is known from the Mousterian levels at Pech de l'Azé in France *c.* 35 000 B.C.

In Egypt cosmetic palettes are found from predynastic times onwards, sometimes perforated for suspension, and finely carved examples occur in alabaster and limestone, which seem to have been the preferred raw materials. At the site of Umm-El-Biyara, in south east Jordan, a stone palette was found engraved with a design of *Tricadna squamosa* lamellibranch shells, a species found in both the Red Sea and the Indian Ocean. Actual incised examples of such shells are widely known from Greece and the Middle East, and were also probably used as toilet utensils. The prehistoric cultures of Egypt and the Middle East have provided most of the actual preserved examples of cosmetics, together with the occasional survival of 'recipes' made of complex (and frequently bizarre) ingredients.

Cosmetic types include eye paints, face paints, oils and solid fats (for ointment and rubs), and in Egyptian times their use was both hygienic and magico-religious. Oils served to protect the skin against the fierce Egyptian sun, functioning as an ultra-violet light barrier in the same way that lotions and oils do today, and they were also used for anointing and rubbing the body after bathing. The widespread use of cosmetics by most social classes generated the manufacture of a series of beautiful vases and boxes, as well as the palettes already mentioned, frequently made of alabaster. Theophrastus, in the 4th century BC, writes, 'Perfumes are ruined by a hot season or by being out in the sun. That is why perfumers seek upper rooms which do not face the sun but which are shaded as much as possible. . . . This is why men put them into vessels of lead and try to secure phials of alabaster, a stone which has the required effect: for lead is cold and of close texture and stone has the same character' (*De Lapidibus*, 65). Pliny (*Natural History*, 36.63) also refers to this property of alabaster, mentioning the fact that onyx marble is sometimes mistakenly called alabaster, 'and may be hollowed out and used as unguent jars as it is said to be the best way of keeping the contents fresh'. Most of the unguents, perfumes and cosmetics used in the ancient world had a vegetable base, but the fats were derived from animals. Many beauty preparations also utilised milk (e.g. Cleopatra's famous bath of asses' milk), honey (good for the complexion), salts and aromatic gums and resins.

Eye paints were a favourite type of Egyptian cosmetic, generally based on malachite (a green copper carbonate, $Cu_2CO_3(OH)_2$) or galena (a dark grey lead ore, PbS). Malachite, certainly known from predynastic times onwards, came principally from Sinai and the eastern desert. It was also used to decorate both male and female skeletons at Çatal Hüyük. Galena, which did not become popular until later periods but continued in use until Coptic times (3rd century AD) came from sources near Aswan and on the Red Sea coast. Both materials have been found in graves, often in small linen or leather bags, or as fragments on palettes and grinding-stones. The prepared cosmetic, usually a mass of finely ground mineral made into a paste, has generally shrunk or is now represented only by dry powder. Sometimes stored in hollow reeds, or wrapped in layers of leaves, it was made up by mixing with water or gum and water, but not with fats, except in the case of kohl face paints. Other, less fashionable eye paints included lead carbonate, black copper oxide, antimony sulphide and crysocolla (a greenish blue copper ore mineral, $CuSiO_3.2H_2O$). These are all 'local' products, except for antimony salts which came from parts of Persia and Asia Minor. Egyptian records state that eye paint was obtained in 12th Dynasty (20th to 13th century BC) times from Asia, in 18th Dynasty times from the as yet unlocated land of 'Punt', and in 19th Dynasty times (14th to 13th century BC) from Coptos (in Lower Egypt), so clearly it formed a sufficiently valuable item of merchandise to be traded at some distance. It has often been suggested that all Egyptian cosmetic preparations contained antimony, but this is manifestly not the case. The Romans, however, used an antimony compound both as an eye cosmetic and an eye medicine, which Pliny (Books 23, 33 and 34) called *stimmi* or *stibi*. Manganese compounds obtained from Sinai were occasionally used as eye paint, although more commonly as a black pigment for tomb painting, or to give a purple colour to glass and glazes.

Until 11th Dynasty times (22nd to 20th century BC) eye paints seem to have been applied with the finger, or with small rods, moistened and then dipped into the dry powder. There seems to have been no call for the ancient equivalent of eye-shadow brushes, dipped dry into the powder, or for fine brushes to draw lines and accentuate the contours of the eye. The exaggerated eyes which appear in so many paintings and sculptures seem to suggest that the Egyptians wore their eye paints far thicker than we do today, and the eye paints were worn by both men and women. The modern variety of kohl which is still used in the East today is often a far cheaper product made of soot (burnt safflower, *Carthamus tinctomus*) and although the use of this and other cosmetics is suggested for a large number of prehistoric communities, nowhere is the archaeological evidence preserved as it has been in Egypt.

A natural corollary of the use of pigments to colour the body is the desire to ornament it with the addition of jewellery. Some form of jewellery has been worn from the very earliest Palaeolithic times, the earliest pieces being made from simple, easily worked materials such as shell, bone and amber. As technological skill increases so does the variety of raw material which can be worked, and the shell necklaces of prehistoric times are replaced by the engraved gemstones of the Classical world.

Amber has been a raw material favoured by numerous different cultures, for its colour, distinctive aroma and rarity value. It is a fossil resin produced by extinct pine trees, generally yellow to brown in colour and translucent to cloudy in texture. It becomes darker, eventually a dark red-brown, on exposure to light and air, by light-induced oxidation. The nature of amber was realised comparatively early, and Pliny remarked that it 'originated as a liquid exudation' and that it contained the remains of ants, gnats and even lizards which were trapped within it before solidification. It is found particularly in Cretaceous and Tertiary rocks, the main source area for European amber being the Baltic, although secondary sources are known in Galicia, Romania and Sicily. It is a common luxury item found in graves in Italy, Greece, Crete and Egypt, from Bronze Age times onwards. Navarro postulated the existence of an amber 'route' during the early and middle Bronze Age, using river transport from west Jutland across Germany finally reaching the Po and the headland of the Adriatic. He thought it likely that the trade was conducted by central European 'middlemen', who could exchange metal for amber. Amber beads were common throughout Bronze Age Europe. In the Iron Age a 'route' started which seems to have terminated at Picenium, where an indigenous amber industry is found in the 6th century BC. Since the days of Helm the succinic acid content of amber has been taken as a guide to establishing the geological origin of amber finds made in archaeological contexts. This component was first detected in Baltic amber, and the recognition of its presence in artefacts used as one of the bases for suggesting amber 'routes'. Helm had the preconceived idea that only Baltic amber contained succinic acid, but it is now thought that its presence is indicative

Figure 21. (1) Amber space-plate necklace from a bowl barrow at Upton Lovell, Wiltshire; Wessex culture. (2) Compound necklace of shale, amber and imported segmented faience beads, from a bell barrow; Wessex culture. Reproduced by kind permission of Miss L. Lewis, Bath Academy of Art and Devizes Museum.

of the state of ageing of the amber, not of its geological origin, and that the so-called amber 'routes' are largely fictitious. It is, however, certain that Baltic amber was traded southwards, but the source of the earliest amber is still an open controversy. The latest laboratory research, using gas-chromatography, indicated that Baltic amber was closer to *Agnathis* (Kauri-gum) resin than to *Pinus* (pine) resin. The characteristic chromatogram now permits Baltic, Rumanian and Sicilian ambers to be distinguished.

Figure 21 shows two necklaces incorporating amber beads, both from the early Bronze Age 'Wessex' culture of southern England. The left-hand example is the famous necklace from a bowl barrow at Upton Lovell (Wiltshire) made from perforated plates and beads of amber, and below it is a compound necklace of shale, amber and imported segmented faience beads from a bell barrow in the same locality. According to Hoare, the original excavator, it once consisted of 5 shale, 27 amber and 16 segmented faience beads, so the illustrated reconstruction probably bears little resemblance to the original form of the necklace. The elaborate multi-strand necklace, the strings separated by space beads with complex perforations, is one of the finest extant examples of amber jewellery, and very similar space-bead necklaces appear in some of the Shaft Graves at Mycenae. The other necklace is possibly later in date. The so-called 'Royal' graves of the Wessex Culture contain burials of warrior chiefs associated with very rich grave goods, beautifully made prestige weapons and ornaments of gold, jet, bronze and amber. A recent study of the Wessex goldwork has demonstrated that all of it could have been the product of one workshop. It would indeed be interesting to know whether the method of distribution and trade of amber objects functioned along the same lines.

The earliest amber artifacts in the Classical world are the Shaft Graves necklaces, but very few finds have been made from contemporary contexts in Minoan Crete. Single amber beads continued to be imported into Greece during the late Helladic period, but very little is found in contexts postdating 550 BC. Amber was imported into Greece by the Phoenician merchants, probably from the Baltic, and was extensively traded by sea routes. The Roman world, on the other hand, obtained amber as a fashionable and expensive luxury from the north via land routes, the main centre of amber carving being Aquileia. Pliny tells us that amber held an important place as a luxury object 'although as yet it is fancied only by women' (*Natural History* 37.11). Tacitus, in 'Germania', noted that lumps of amber were gathered by the natives from the sea shore and forwarded to Rome unshaped. The tribesmen were apparently astonished to be paid for it, and no doubt such credulity was thoroughly exploited by the Roman entrepreneurs. Pliny also quotes a story about a knight who was commanded by the emperor Nero to bring back a cargo of amber to make ornaments for a display of gladiators. He returned with such a large quantity that even the nets used to keep the animals from the parapet of the amphitheatre were knotted with it and there was still sufficient to ornament the arms and biers of the gladiators. The heaviest lump brought back weighed 13 lb (5.9 kg). Juvenal records that the Romans liked to hold a piece of amber in their hands, because of the pleasant smell (*Satires*, VI.573–4). The so-called 'worry-beads' (*sibha*, or *mosibha*) used in Moslem countries are often made of amber for the same reason, and perfectly matched strings have become collectors' items. Strings of 99 or 101 beads are used for religious purposes to count off prayers, but these are never made of amber, but of a black variety of stone. Amber beads are used for necklaces, as well as for *sibha*, and in Greece the custom of using the equivalent of *sibha*, κομπόλοι (kompoloi) seems to have been imported from Turkey.

Fossils, especially teeth and shells, are another group of raw materials much employed by early man for the first types of jewellery. Sharks' teeth have attracted attention from lower Palaeolithic times, and, being durable, are often preserved in archaeological contexts. At the Aurignacian site of Tuc d'Audoubert, a painted cave in the Pyrenean foothills, specimens were found which must have been brought a distance of at least 94 miles (150 km), and then perforated for stringing. Wearing perforated teeth is a very common trait among primitive people even in the present day, and thought to give the hunter some of the attributes of the source animal, generally a carnivore. Figure 22 shows a collection of such teeth from a necklace at a Grimaldian burial (*c.* 12 000 BC) at Balzi Rossi (Ventimiglia, N. Italy). The Upper Palaeolithic cultures living in Moravia at about the same time wore necklaces of canine teeth strung together with *Dentalium* shells (narrow, tube-shaped marine gastropods). These also appear in the aceramic Neolithic cultures of Palestine, and seem to have been extensively traded in prehistoric Europe. A necklace of 20 fossil *Dentalium* shells is illustrated in Figure 23, from a flat bowl barrow of Bronze Age date at Winterbourne Stoke, Wiltshire. The shells seem to have been associated originally with the bones of a sheep, and since the barrow also contained other ornaments, 48 clay disc beads and 3 stem-ossicles of a fossil

Figure 22. Necklace of deer teeth and various shells from a Grimaldian burial at Balzi Rossi (Ventimiglia), N. Italy. Reproduced by kind permission of Saprintendenza alle antechità della Liguria.

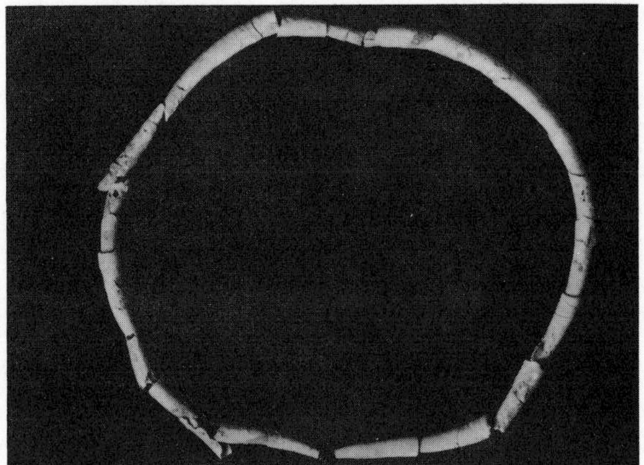

Figure 23. Necklace of 20 *Dentalium* shells from a Bronze Age barrow at Winterbourne Stoke, Wiltshire. (Photo, Nick Pollard)

crinoid, it is possible that the necklace was originally both compound and much larger. These crinoid stem fragments are common in Carboniferous or Jurassic limestones, and have given their names to the distinctive crinoidal marble, correctly crinoidal limestone, a popular building stone. Short lengths of crinoid stem have been found in a number of different barrows, and appear to have been sought after since they form such convenient beads. It is possible that the form of the segmented faience beads (Fig. 21, p. 106), much used as trade objects in the Bronze Age and common in the Wessex culture, was originally modelled on a crinoid stem, since the shapes are almost identical.

Shell necklaces, pendants, amulets and girdles are (inevitably) common in Egypt from predynastic times onwards, and the employment of larger shells as cosmetic containers has already been mentioned, (p. 106). The majority of the shells used came from the Red Sea, although Mediterranean species, freshwater shells from the Nile and the occasional land shell also turn up. Beads were made by breaking the shell into suitably sized pieces, trimming them along the edge and drilling the hole from both sides with a blunt point. The results were finished off by final smoothing along the edges, probably after stringing. They went out of use or fashion at some time during the 18th Dynasty, and were replaced by similarly shaped beads made of faience. The tomb of Tutankhamun contained thousands of beads but none made of shell. Shell beads came back into use and regained their popularity in the 19th Dynasty, and were still much used at the time of the 22nd (935 BC).

There seems to have been a well-established trade in recent sea shells even in Palaeolithic times, Mediterranean and Atlantic shells from the coast being traded inland into southern France, and sometimes combined there with fossil shells from local sources. Fossil gastropods were especially popular for Palaeolithic jewellery, probably because they were stronger than brachiopod shells after piercing. Brachiopods were, however, used by the mammoth hunters of Vestonice, and a necklace partly composed of fossil *Terebratula* has been found. The length of the Upper Palaeolithic trade routes in fossil shells can be illustrated by the fact that two of the gastropods found in a Magdalenian layer at Laugerie Basse (Dordogne) can be matched, as far as is known, only from the Eocene deposits of the Isle of Wight.

An eccentric form of jewellery is the prehistoric arrowhead, particularly Upper Palaeolithic and Beaker varieties. These seem to have been mounted and worn as amulets from Medieval times onwards, and only recently a reputable and expensive firm of jewellers advertised brooches, rings and sleeve links of gold, set with small arrowheads and microliths, although presumably for decorative rather than protective purposes. More than one well-known museum has a profitable side line in selling off unprovenanced (and thus archaeologically useless) arrowheads set as brooches and cuff-links, a useful source of finance in days of economic stringency.

Stone beads and necklaces have always been popular, made by roughly shaping natural crystals and pebbles, and then smoothing by rubbing if the exterior surface was not intended to be left rough. In Egypt the beads were then pierced and glazed, the hole being bored from either one or two sides, the drill diameter being $\frac{1}{8}$ in. (3 mm). The drill itself, either made of copper or of a hard vegetable stalk, was operated by a bow using quartz or emery as an abrasive, and the process is shown very clearly in some 18th-Dynasty tomb paintings in the Theban necropolis. Quartz sand is a more likely choice as an abrasive than emery, since it was locally available and would cut all the stones worked except beryl, which could be cut by its own dust. A similar technique was in use on the other side of the world, in the Aztec culture of Central America, where the use of tubular drills of bone or reed has already been mentioned. Aztec jewellery also made much use of shell, set in mosaic with turquoise, iron pyrites, jade, emerald and opals, and laid on a backing of clay, wood or reed. Favourite shapes included elaborately wrought plugs for earlobes, necklaces and bracelets for arms and legs, nose ornaments, and pendants to be hung from the lower lip. Diadems of gold, jade or turquoise were worn as badges of office. Aztec lapidary technique was amazingly advanced, very hard and very delicate materials being worked with equal skill.

The faience beads mentioned above, were made of finely ground glazed quartz, and it has been suggested that this process was discovered accidentally by a fire in a sand dune or in the course of copper smelting. The manufacture of faience is a process almost peculiar to Egypt, the beads consisting of a core, with a coating of vitreous alkaline glaze. The body material is always granular and often friable, generally white in colour but sometimes brown, green or yellowish. Occasionally a very slight blue or green tinge may be seen, due to impurities in the material. The glaze covering is typically blue, green or greeny-blue, occasionally violet, white or yellow, and is composed of a sodium–calcium–silicate glass or a potassium–calcium–silicate glass. The proportion of lime is lower and the percentage of silica higher than in modern glass. The colour comes from a copper compound, and the alkali is derived from plant ash, not from natron (p. 130). The faience products (beads are the most common), were made in various types of moulds. One form had a narrow channel across the edge near the top of the mould, where a thick copper wire was placed. The mould was then filled with powdered quartz to above the level of the wire, which, after firing, could be removed, leaving a perforation through the object for suspension. Occasionally some of the larger faience objects were wheel turned, especially thin bowls and large jars, while a few of the poorer-quality products were formed solid and then hollowed out while the quartz paste was still wet. If a green glaze was required a yellowish-tinted body was tried under a blue glaze. Black faience is known but is very rare, the colour being derived from copper oxide.

The scarab, called after the scarab beetle (Latin, *Scarabaeus* sp.) is associated with Egypt, although it was a form of jewellery equally popular with the Etruscans. Egyptian examples retain to the last the beetle form, and early examples often have carvings of animals on the reverse. The Romans adopted the scarab from the Etruscans. Some scarabs were made of faience, but the majority were cut out of steatite or calcareous schists, or, more rarely, basalt, carnelian and lapis lazuli. Rough shaping was done by filing with emery or quartz sand, and any subsequent engraving carried out using flint tools. Lines of hieroglyphics, often crudely engraved, may cover the flat base and the resulting stone was often used as a seal. Almost all the Etruscan scarabs are made of carnelian (or sard, a brown carnelian), red or reddish-brown in colour. The name comes from the Latin *cornum*, a red berry, but the false etymology derives it from *carnis* (flesh), which has popularised the misspelling of carnelian. Greek scarabs are made of a wider variety of gems, including emeralds and amber, but red carnelian still seems to have been favoured. The earliest method of wearing such a seal was to string it with other beads as a necklace, so that the engraved base could be used as a seal. When the stone was mounted for a finger ring a wire was passed through a longitudinal perforation of the stone, and then through holes in a gold band or a band of plaited wire. The ends of the loop were often ornamented and formed into discs to secure the stone.

Assyrian and Persian seals were generally cylindrical or barrel-shaped, up to 2 in. (5 cm) long and up to 1 in. (2.5 cm)

Figure 24. Green chalcedony Persian cylinder seal carved with a scene and the name DARIUS. The impression made by the seal is shown on the right. Reproduced by kind permission of the Trustees of the British Museum.

wide. String was passed through a large hole in the middle and the seal then tied round the wrist as a bracelet. Favoured raw materials again included carnelian and lapis lazuli, together with jasper, chalecedony and agate. Religious motifs and scenes of man-and-beast contests are the most common. Figure 24 shows a green chalcedony Persian seal, carved with the name DARIUS. The impression made by the seal is on the right hand side, and was made by rolling it over a lump of tempered clay laid on the object or join for which a seal was required. This particular seal is very well known, and is thought to have belonged to the Great King himself. Although in the ancient world a seal was customarily either held in the hand or worn as a bracelet or necklace, as already indicated, Old Testament references to seals always describe them as being held in the hand, never on the finger. The signet ring seems to have been a Greek invention at some time before 600 BC, a date at which the lawgiver Solon passed a regulation prohibiting gem engravers from keeping the impressions of any signet once sold, in order to prevent the production of replicas.

Plain rings carved from stone were popular in Roman times, frequently made of chalcedony and sometimes of jasper. Oriental stone rings were made of similar materials, but tended to be much larger in size, designed to be worn on the thumb of the right hand in order to be used in drawing the bowstring. Oriental bows were pulled with the bent thumb, catching it against the shank of the ring, not with the two fingers as in English archery.

Both jet and shale were popular for jewellery in Iron Age and Roman Britain although they are uncommon in other cultures. Jet is found in the Upper Lias of Yorkshire, particularly in the Whitby area, exposed on the coast between Ravenscar and Port Mulgrave. It was worked into bracelets, rings and pins, production being established at least by the 7th century BC. In Roman times jet carving was a small-scale luxury trade, the substance being prized for its attractive appearance and electrostatic properties, in addition to any rarity value. Figure 25 shows a Roman pendant made from Whitby jet, bearing a rather attractive family portrait shown in relief. The industry seems to have exported most of its products,

Figure 25. Romano-British pendant made from Whitby jet, bearing an attractive family portrait. Reproduced by kind permission of the Yorkshire Museum.

particularly to the Rhineland, where many finds have been reported but the lack of any form of manufacturing waste supports the theory that the objects arrived from England ready-made.

A similar industry was based on Kimmeridge shale, which occurs in the Isle of Purbeck (Dorset), and outcrops in the cliff as a dark brown, black or grey oily rock (Fig. 26). The shale is rather soft and soapy in texture, and was used as the basis for quite an extensive manufacturing industry producing jewellery and other objects, from Iron Age times right through the Roman period. Slabs of shale were quarried from the cliffs and taken up to nearby occupation sites for working. The settlement at Eldons Seat (Encombe, Dorset) produced evi-

Figure 26. Outcrops of brown shale in the cliffs at Kimmeridge Bay, Dorset.

dence of the complete process. The initial slab was divided into discs, using flint knives, and a central core removed to make a ring, which was slowly ground down into bracelets, armlets, anklets and pendants. In the 1st century AD lathe-turning techniques were introduced, which required two or three holes to be bored in the shale disc, enabling it to be fitted onto pegs on a wooden chuck. This technique seems to have resulted in the production of a wider range of goods, even trays and three-legged tables, the legs of the latter being decorated with lion or gryphon heads and claws, in imitation of Italian marble and bronze furniture. Such objects are, however, rather uncommon, and many of the shale products have a fairly localised distribution within a radius of 40 miles (64 km) from Purbeck. The shale source had been exploited sporadically as early as Beaker times, for the manufacture of V-perforated buttons, toggles and rings. In the Wessex culture these buttons sometimes had gold covers made for them, as in the beautiful example shown from Upton Lovell, in Wiltshire (Fig. 27 (1)), where the grooved ornament of the gold cover is repeated on the shale core.

Gemstones of different types have exerted a peculiar fascination over all cultures and periods, related most probably to their immanent beauty rather than to their intrinsic value. Often a gem may be considered a work of art, when it has been engraved or set, but certainly the beauty of the stone always made it a highly prized object conferring status on the wearer. As a result a vast mythology has grown up surrounding gem-

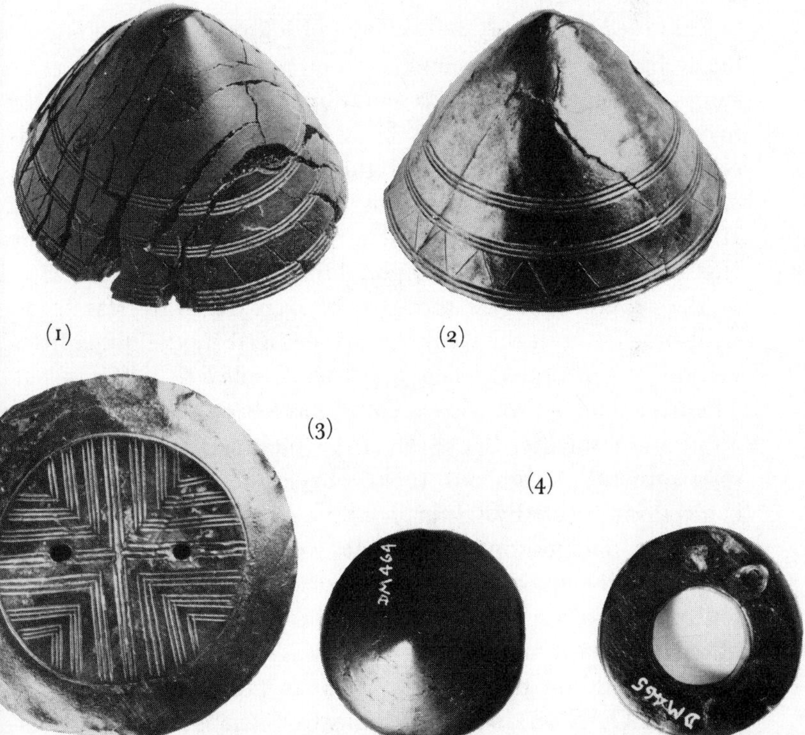

Figure 27. (1)–(3) Conical shale button with gold cover, Wessex culture. The ornament on the gold cover is reproduced on the shale. (4) V-perforated shale button and toggle, Beaker culture. (Photo, Nick Pollard).

stones especially in relation to their supposed magical properties and the legends associated with them. Frequently a 'bad luck' tag is attached to the possession of particular stones, such as the 'moonstone' of Wilkie Collins, or the recurrent association of certain types of gemstones with nebulous un-named far-Eastern temples. This last myth recurs in literature from Goethe to Agatha Christie. Apart from the beauty of stones their value also depends on other properties like the electrostatic nature of jet and amber, or the degree to which they reflect or concentrate light. Legends about the magical or religious significance of gems and their colours persist right down to the present day, with the popularity of rings or pendants set with 'birthstones', and the still-extant superstition that it is unlucky to wear an opal.

Engraved gems may be a source of information on domestic life, religious rites or weapons, as in Etruscan or Greek gemstones with their exact representations of armour. Much of the mystique of Mithraism has been culled from gems and bas reliefs, and our knowledge of the history of Egypt has been amplified by the scarabs bearing the names and titles of kings. It is extremely unfortunate that neither the wearing nor the engraving of gemstones was popular in prehistoric times. Most of the stones used by the Greeks were, by our standards, semi-precious, but their value was enhanced by the difficulty of working them and the fact that they needed to be imported. Their particular favourites seem to have been beryl (beryllium aluminium silicate, $Be_3Al_2(Si_6O_{18})$ which occurs as an accessory mineral in igneous rocks, chrysoprase (an apple-green chalcedony), amethyst (purple or violet-coloured quartz) and carnelian. The most precious stones were the hardest, since they presented the maximum amount of difficulty in cutting and setting, and these tended to be avoided until after the time of Alexander. Some stones which were not hard to work were prized for their rarity, such as lapis lazuli (lazurite, $3(NaAlSiO_4)Na_2S$), obtainable only from the mines of Afghanistan. Several classical authors mention gemstones in passing, but the most useful work is undoubtedly that of Theophrastus, who lists the kinds of gems used in the Roman world in his own times. He mentioned the use of turquoise, which was, however, more favoured by the Persians for charms and amulets. It has the unfortunate property of decaying rapidly with exposure to excess light or moisture, and is thus not well represented in archaeological contexts. There is a Medieval legend that the stone would grow pale on the finger of a sick person, recovering its colour if transferred to a healthy hand. Ancient engraved turquoises are very rare indeed, and the original blue has almost always been converted to a dull green by oxidation of the copper. Carnelian, mentioned above (p. 112), was particularly favoured by nearly all ancient gem engravers for its pleasant red tones. It is common on beaches in all parts of Europe, especially where the beach is composed of rolled flint pebbles. The oldest Etruscan and Egyptian intaglios were cut upon this stone, which has the advantages of being tough and easy to work, and which retains a high polish, so Pliny says, longer than any other gem. Harder stones like garnet often have their surfaces scratched by wear.

Opal (hydrous silica, $SiO_2.nH_2O$) is another stone which does not occur frequently in archaeological contexts, and it seems to have been both rare and very highly prized in the Classical world. The most famous opal in history was that owned by the Roman senator Nonius, which was reputed to be the size of a hazel nut and valued at 2 million sesterces (*c.* £300 000). Mark Antony, who coveted the stone, threatened to exile the senator, who preferred to accept the exile rather than relinquish the opal. In the present day opals are obtained principally from Australian mines, the most expensive variety being the pure white opal, and not the blue 'sandwich' stone. The opal is still regarded as unlucky and it is certainly a very brittle stone, cracking on exposure to sudden heat and losing its beauty during wear due to a coat of dust and grease. This is possibly the reason for the legend, since sudden uneven expansion as a result of heating can cause the opal to fall out of its setting, and the rather fragile nature of the stone itself does not indicate a long life span for it as a jewel.

Gemstones can be engraved by using the wheel, a small copper disc fixed on to the end of a spindle and moved by a lathe. The fine edge is moistened with oil, emery or diamond dust, and can be used to cut the hardest gems. This method was first employed in the time of the emperor Domitian, and thus is not mentioned by Pliny. A drill can be substituted for the cutting disc, and worked by hand by means of a bow in the same way that a cube is rotated to cut stone. Gems can also be cut using a diamond point, produced by splitting a diamond with a blow from a heavy hammer and fitting the point to the end of an iron tool. Gemstones were usually polished by the Romans with emery (a grey-black variety of corundum) obtained from Naxos, but Indian gems seem to have been polished with a mixture of oil and emery on an iron slab, a process used even for diamonds.

Bloodstone (a red-speckled form of chalcedony) was favoured by the Romans, and called 'heliotrope' from the belief that if immersed in water it reflected an image of the sun bright red in colour. Two sorts of red jasper were also known, one of a rich crimson especially liked for imperial portraits. Agate (a variegated chalcedony found filling the vesicles in amygdeloidal volcanic rocks) was used as a gemstone both for its attractive colour and the belief that it was an antidote to snake bite. Garnets (common minerals in metamorphic rocks) do not often occur as engraved gems, except in Persia, since the wax tends to stick to them in sealing. One famous garnet was a pendant in the regalia of Mary Queen of Scots, and was valued in those days at the enormous sum of 500 crowns. Modern engravers also seldom use garnet, since it is difficult to work and inclined to be rather brittle. The Romans made more use of sapphires (another form of corundum) after the development of larger-scale trading with India at the time of the emperor Trajan (early 2nd century AD) since one of the major sources of the stone, both then and in the present day, is the island of Sri Lanka. The ancient name of the stone, Hyacinthus, was derived from its colour resemblance to the flower supposed to have sprung from the blood of the dead boy of the same name, accidentally killed by Apollo. The ruby is not so hard a stone, but carved rubies are even rarer than carved sapphires, the stones being generally set in rings and jewellery polished but uncut. Topaz (aluminium fluorsilicate $Al_2F_2SiO_4$) was obtained from the Red Sea region, and is one of the softest precious stones. It was found in pieces of such size that the Egyptian Queen Arsinoë (1st century BC) had a statue of herself carved out of a single gem. The stone was usually set transparently by the Romans, who had the habit of setting other stones surrounded by a red foil of copper and gold (aurich alcum), a forerunner of the cloissoné technique popular in the Dark Ages.

The emerald (a chromium-rich variety of beryl) is another stone which is uncommon in antiquity, although a superb example was reputedly in the possession of the Frankish Queen Theodelinda at the end of the 6th century AD. Pliny says that Bactrian and Scythian stones were considered to be the best, from their dark colour and freedom from flaws, but that they were too hard to be engraved. The chief source of emeralds for the Roman world was, however, Egyptian mines near Coptos. Nero was reputedly the owner of an enormous emerald, which he used as a glass to view gladiatorial contests, since he was extremely short sighted. The Romans considered looking at an emerald to be beneficial to the sight, and it is suggested that this stone may also have been hollowed out at the back, thus acting as a concave lens to magnify the distant scene.

The diamond was never itself engraved, in either ancient or modern times, but was instead used as an engraving tool. Great value has been set on diamonds since Classical times. The mantle of Charlemagne was fastened with four large diamonds forming a clasp, thought to be of Roman origin. Many intriguing legends have grown up around diamonds, especially those of large size or peculiar shape, the most valuable being pure white in colour. Many times the legends have seemed to be coming true, as in the case of the Hindu superstition that the Koh-i-Nor diamond would bring ruin to the person or dynasty possessing it. The 17th-century Mogul dynasty who owned it gradually declined, and India was later lost to the British crown soon after the stone was presented to Queen Victoria by Lord Dalhousie. Like all such tales the glamour surrounding the stone is mixed with a kind of superstitious awe, and an 800 carat diamond stimulated unparalleled greed and envy, itself a source of crime and a creator of more legends.

There has never been a human community which did not indulge itself in some form of personal adornment, from the simple shell necklace of Palaeolithic times to the engraved gemstones of the Classical world. This progression is cultural as well as technological, and is also dependent on subsidiary factors such as fashion and trade efficiency. The desire to enhance personal appeal and increase status is as old as humanity itself, and it is indeed sad that only sporadic archaeological evidence of so human a trait has been preserved.

CHAPTER 6

Medicine and technology

'Progress celebrates Pyrrhic victories over Nature'

(Karl Kraus)

It is a remarkable truth that the savants of the ancient world, while making important discoveries in mathematics and astronomy, did not make similar progress in the field of the natural sciences. This seems to be a consequence of the common belief that all natural phenomena were originally created and were still being manipulated by mythical deities of uncertain temper. Classical philosophers such as Heraclitus (*c.* 500 BC), and Empedocles, writing a little later, were responsible for the evolution of the concept of the four basic elements (earth, air, fire and water), which was to last for nearly 2000 years during which true science, as such, languished. The Medieval idea that the earth had been recently created and would soon come to an end was a development of the Christian philosophical explanation of 'why' things happened, making it irrelevant to know 'how'. Since the earth did not end people at length realised that it might be worth collecting facts about it, and the new interest in science and technology which characterised the Renaissance was responsible for the development of many ideas which would formerly have been thought revolutionary. For geology, at any rate, it was not until the principles of stratigraphy and evolution had been formalised by Lyell and Darwin that the maze of superstition, legend and speculation could be replaced by anything more concrete. It is therefore understandable that in Classical and Medieval times, and even more so in any prehistoric culture, the practice of medicine and technology were naturally inextricably linked with ritual and religion. Observation of natural phenomena cannot, in such a climate of thought, be objective, and it would have been impossible for the ancients to envisage a scientific or technological process as able to function without at least some degree of supernatural control. As Robert Graves says, through the mouth of the emperor Claudius, in his delightful reconstruction of life in 1st century Rome 'Medicine mixed and taken without prayers would have seemed as unlucky and useless as a wedding celebrated without guests'. In Classical Greece, for example, theory and abstract argument were preferable to practice, and in spite of a high level of craftsmanship technology was virtually stagnant. There was little interest in experimental evidence and still less in practical applications. In medicine, too, little progress was made, except for the gradual rise of the cult of the god of healing (Asclepios), whose principal sanctuary was near Epidauros and whose cures seem to have been effected by a combination of faith and common sense. Greek medicine was not, however, as tied to priestcraft as it had been in many earlier societies, and in archaic Greece doctors enjoyed a wide reputation. The enlightened school of thought established following Hippocrates of Cos (5th century) relied on the use of plant extracts as drugs.

Even today there are a number of superstitions connected with medical, culinary and technological matters which persist not only amongst the less well educated. One thinks of the habit of tossing a pinch of salt over the left shoulder to blind the devil who is supposed to stand there (a relic of the day when salt was a valuable commodity); the belief that it is unlucky for a woman to go down a mine; or the numerous wrongly held ideas about home medicinal remedies. Leonardus Camillus wrote a book about precious stones in the 18th century, where he described the characteristics and powers of the gems. The stones often combined the function of jewel, amulet, medicine, prophylactic and placebo, and in the mind of the writer it would no doubt have been impossible to disassociate one from the other.

A similar set of values was held in the ancient world, the Sumerians being a case in point. They possessed a rich variety of technological learning by the 4th millennium BC, having already discovered writing, initiated some simple chemistry and co-operated on monumental building works. In common with Egypt they did not, however, possess scientific curiosity as we know it today, but had a unifying philosophy of speculative thought which did not always separate the underlying abstractions from their rational beliefs. The practice of technology was, of course, closely connected to other fields such as astronomy, mathematics and astrology, and the aid of the supernatural was often invoked in a chemical process. Levey quotes as an example a 7th century BC Assyrian chemist who carried out a sacrifice of embryos to aid him in the manufacture of glass. This close link between technology and magic survived until comparatively recently in the efforts of the alchemists.

During the Archaic period in Egypt the bond between science and superstition is manifested in a particularly striking way in their medical discoveries, but few medical treatises have any sort of empirical basis. An Egyptian medical student needed to be able to learn the various prescriptions, spells and diagnoses contained in the medical papyri, which varied in quality from a collection of medico-religious recipes often utilising mineral substances, to quasi-scientific treatises on surgery and fractures. Our present knowledge of Mesopotamian medicine and chemical technology is again derived from contemporary literature, supplemented by evidence from artefacts and the writings of succeeding civilisations. Contemporary literature includes Phoenician and Ugaritic sources, together with some Hittite cuneiforms, but the most important sources are the Sumerian and Akkadian tablets themselves. These include lists of stores and provisions, bills of sale and recipes, a lexical list of drugs, spices and minerals. Their literature is rich in material dealing with history, ritual and omens, and includes descriptions of the practical application of a number of chemicals, those used, for example, in the salting of a corpse for its preservation, or details of the preparation of oils and perfumes. As in Egypt many ailments were thought to have been caused

Figure 28. Two Assyrian cuneiform medical texts utilising mineral substances. Original texts on clay tablets. After Rawlinson (1891).

by evil demons, and magic was therefore a more effective method of treatment than medicine. Both cultures have left recipes for the prescription of drugs, interspersed with prayers and spells suitable for reciting while the drug was being administered.

Certain mineral substances used for quasi-medicinal purposes recur in the pharmacopoeia of several civilisations, alum being a good example. Potash alum ($KAl(SO_4)_2.12H_2O$) is found naturally in an octahedral crystalline form, and can also be obtained by roasting the so-called alumstone ($KAl_3(SO_4)_2(OH)_6$) in air and recrystallising. It is used in tanning, dyeing, glass making and medicine, particularly for treatment of diseases of the head, eyes and ears. Figure 28 shows part of an Assyrian cuneiform text, which was translated by Thomsen, 'If a man and his eyes are troubled with blood dropping, . . . alum, tannin together thou shalt rub . . . thou shalt wash, knead, roast in an oven . . . [and apply]' (Text K11695).

Alum was imported into Mesopotamia from an as yet unidentified country called Kesabbu, and also from Egypt where it was still being produced from quarries in Upper Egypt in the

15th century AD. The literature also records alum as having been imported from the Hittites in Asia Minor in the late 2nd millennium BC, and there were, in addition, some minor local sources. References in the literature include several in the tablets of Nebuchadnezzar. Alum was sometimes used in combination with very unsavoury mixtures of substances, as in Text K2532 (Fig. 28), whose curative properties must have been minimal; it is perhaps fortunate that faith can move mountains. The translation of this text is another general prescription for diseases of the head '. . . leek, an old shoe, together thou shalt dry, reduce . . . lead, antimony, salt together thou shalt mix, once, twice, or thrice. . . . If ditto alum and chamomile thou shalt bray, in cedar oil mix, apply to his head and he shall recover'.

A third 'recipe' Text K2570, is specifically for diseases of the eyes. 'If a man's eyes are sick and matter is secreted on his temples thou shalt spread tanners verdigris on vellum, on his eyes, bind: bray copper dust, arsenic, yellow sulphide of arsenic mix in curd, apply to his eyes . . .'.

Blanks in the texts occur where the tablet is unreadable, and some of the instances used are as yet unidentified. The arsenic would probably have been obtained from the ore arsenopyrite (FeAsS), but the composition of 'tanners verdigris' is not known. Alum was also used in the treatment of jaundice and as a mouthwash, and even (when mixed with cedar oil) as a yellow hair dye. Technological uses included wood fireproofing, as a flux to solder copper and in metallurgy to separate gold and silver. It was also extensively used in leather processing, and Reed (p. 154) quotes a Mesopotamian text of 800 BC giving instruction for dressing a freshly-slaughtered oxhide.

'This skin you will take it
Then you will drench it in pure pulverised Nisaba flour,
in water, beer and first quality wine,
with the best fat of a pure ox
the alum of the land of the Hittites
and oak-galls will you press it
and you will cover the bronze kettle-drum with it.'

The oak-galls would have been a tanning agent and also assisted in preserving the hide from decomposition.

No actual discovery of alum has been made from an Egyptian achaeological context, although its presence is attested by the circumstantial evidence of the presence of ancient mines. It was almost certainly the mordant to which Pliny refers for fixing the colours during the dyeing of cloth.

The mixture of mineral-derived substances with oils or fats, as in the recipe above, was also a common feature of Roman medicine. Indeed Pliny proposes 'unsalted axle grease . . . mixed with old oil, crushed sarcophagus stone and cinquefoil pounded in wine, or with lime or with ash' as a sovereign remedy for gout (*Natural History*, 28. 39). Other natural substances such as amber also had a medicinal use; Callistratus tells us that it was a remedy for people of any age who were subject to 'attacks of wild distraction', and it was thought by the Romans to cure fevers and diseases, when worn as an amulet on a necklace, infections of the ears when powdered and mixed with honey and rose-oil, and weak sight if powdered and blended with Attic honey. 'Amber, indeed is supposed to be a prophylactic against tonsilitis and other affections of the pharynx, for the water near the Alps has properties that harm the human throat in various ways' (Pliny, 37.44). This last sentence is generally thought to be a reference to goitre.

Fossils, too, hold a place in medical history. *Spirifer*, a Devonian brachiopod, has wings like the outstretched wings of a bird, and from the 4th century onwards these fossils were known in China as 'stone swallows' (Shih-yen). A recent application for Shih-yen made at an apothecary's shop in Singapore produced the specimens shown in Figure 29, together with a leaflet which describes the drug made from them as 'sweet and cooling, good for treating rheumatism, skin diseases and eye troubles' (Oakley, 1965, p. 13). Chinese folklore also records their use in medicine, and one Taoist writer of the 8th century recognised the fact that the 'stone swallows' were really 'sea shells raised on to mountains by catastrophic changes in geography' (Oakley op. cit). The supposed bones and teeth of dragons were also thought in China to have healing powers, since in

Figure 29. 'Stone swallows'. Two Devonian *Spirifer* obtained from an apothecary's shop in Singapore. A leaflet supplied with them described their supposed medicinal properties. Photograph reproduced by kind permission of the Trustees of the British Museum, Natural History.

Chinese tradition the emperor was guarded by a dragon, which was also a bringer of rain in times of drought. Indeed the discovery of the important Lower Palaeolithic cave of Chou K'ou Tien, the type site for the hominid *Sinanthropus pekinensis* (Pekin man) was indirectly the result of the discovery of a fossil hominoid tooth in a collection of 'dragons' teeth' bought in a drugstore earlier this century. Professor G. H. R. von Koenigswald obtained teeth of the extinct hominid *Gigantopithecus* by this means, using one of the attractive Chinese prescriptions for 'dragons' bones', which could of course be any type of large bone which looked old and large enough to be genuine.

Many mineral substances, like alum, found uses both in technology and in medicine, and certainly in the Middle East they were among the earliest materials used in the development of chemistry, due to their availability and frequent occurrence in a fairly pure form. This afforded the experimenters reproducible results, always desirable when working with unknown materials. In Mesopotamia gypsum salt and soda assumed such a position in antiquity. The three are sometimes confused since it is frequently difficult to distinguish precisely which one is being referred to, although the lexical lists of Sumerian and Akkadian literature are a help. All three substances are often used in dyeing, a complex process which requires two agents, one to supply the colour and another (the mordant) to fix the dye into the fabric. In the earliest times a mordant was not used, but at later dates its advantages were realised, and everywhere the most common mordant is alum. In Egypt the dye was generally vegetable in origin, often giving brown, blue or green colours, lime, soda or potash being mixed with the essence to make the dye. The Sumerians dyed wool blue with a mixture of indigo and potash, or with woad (*Isatis tinctonia* L), although in mythology the woad plant seems to be the preserve of the mythical 'Ancient Britons'. Certainly the Celtic tribes of late pre-Roman Europe seem to have used it as a body paint. Cassia bark, which contains much tannic acid, was mixed with iron sulphate to give a black-green dye, and the sumach plant, mixed with the same mineral, gave a black dye. Iron was also required for the production of the famous 'Tyrian purple', a colour obtained from the glands of small molluscs, *Murex*, found on the beaches of Phoenicia, Crete, and Sidon. The glands of these various species of *Murex* were salted, cooked, put in the sun and evaporated, and then generally mordanted with iron and pomegranate rinds. Other mordants included the metallic salts of aluminium and iron, as well as tannins derived from a variety of plants.

Another important salt was natron, a naturally occurring compound of sodium carbonate and sodium bicarbonate. It is found plentifully in Egypt, especially at the Wadi el Natrun, and in the Beheira province of lower Egypt, a source definitely worked in antiquity, and in Ptolemaic times was under Royal monopoly. Egyptian natron nearly always contains salt (sodium chloride) and sodium sulphate as impurities. At Wadi el Natrun it is found dissolved in the lake water, from which a thick layer has gradually been deposited on the bottom of some of the lakes, and also as an encrustation on the ground adjoining the lake. Its numerous uses included ritual purification, the manufacture of incense, glass, glazes and some pigments, together with the bleaching of linen. Pliny mentions a culinary use, 'Egyptian soda (natron) for radishes; it makes them more tender but meats white and inferior and vegetables greener' (*Natural History*, 31.46).

Common salt (sodium chloride, NaCl) has, however, a much wider range of applications than natron, and was used by all prehistoric and modern societies in one form or another. It occurs naturally both as rock salt and as brine (in sea water) and was often very cheap, as in the time of Nebuchadnezzar when one talent of salt could be bought with one shekel of silver. It has been suggested that people's appetite for salt seems to increase with the vegetable component of their food, but this seems to be fairly illogical, since salt was always a vital ingredient in human diet, and its production, distribution and exchange have been major factors in the most efficient prehistoric economies. In Egypt salt was used as a seasoning, in the preparation of food and in mummification, and, like natron, was a Royal monopoly during Ptolemaic times. It has often been erroneously suggested that it was used in mummification as brine solution, as a result of a mistranslation of Herodotus' description of embalming. Used dry it would give better results than when used in solution, and there are many references to the analogies between fish curing, always done with dry salt, and mummification. There is only one reliable instance (the tomb of Hetepheres) of the viscera having been preserved in salt solution. An additional point in favour of its having been used dry is the fact that such a huge bath would have been required for the long-term soaking of the corpse, none have been found nor are any shown in tomb-paintings. In Mesopotamia salt was kept in 'salt bags' when travelling, in salt cellars when at home, or in a special box used for a mixture of salt and mustard which was used as a condiment. As in Egypt it was also used for the preservation of meat and corpses, and had many additional functions in medicine and as one of the ingredients in a blue glaze. Hides were either cured in antiquity by dry salting, covering the fresh pelt with crystalline salt before drying, or by wet salting where a pile of skins was made and then each covered with salt, resulting in strong brine solutions dripping through the skins. After about two weeks the skins were cured and allowed to dry out.

From the earliest times salt has been traded in Europe along well-defined salt routes, together with amber, flint and probably also merchandise such as furs and textiles, which have left no trace in the archaeological record. In Iron Age times both rock salt deposits and saline springs were exploited. The Indo-European place names HAL (as in Halstatt) or WICH (as in Droitwich) refer to old salt producing locations, and the large scale production of salt at such places often begins at a date contemporary with the beginning of iron working. The rock salt mines of the eastern Alps were particularly extensive, galleries being driven hundreds of metres into the mountain and salt extracted using simple tools such as picks, shovels and wedges. By the 7th to 5th centuries BC there were at least fifteen known centres of salt mining in Europe, and probably at least a dozen more in operation. Gaul, curiously, came to have a high reputation for salted products, pork, bacon and hams being exported to the Roman world, and it seems probable that salt trading was an essential part of the economic basis of the Celtic world. Strabo, in his *Geography*, also notes the trade route from Gaul to Italy in salted meat and blankets. Some of the salt mines have preserved finds of textiles and leather, including a miner's leather cap, tunics and knapsacks from Iron Age mines in the Tyrol. Later in time the workmen seem to have abandoned the mining of rock salt, and to have focused their interest on the brine recovered from sumps in the mines, which they concentrated in salterns in the fields in front of the mines. This process was carried out by allowing the brine to trickle over hot stones or clay bars erected over fires, and then directing it into clay troughs.

In pre-Roman times salt had been obtained in England by boiling sea water in vats, a process which was continued and developed after the conquest, especially in the Fenland and East Anglian coasts. There sea water was allowed (probably at the beginning of summer) to flow into large pans which were then covered and left to evaporate until the autumn. The crust of crude salt and the underlying salt-impregnated clay were broken up and roasted in open fires to facilitate the final retrieval of salt from the resulting granular masses by dissolving it out in strong brine solutions. This salt-rich liquor was decanted off and again evaporated in large boiling pans, supported on clay bars. At Ingoldmills on the Lincolnshire coast salt pans 2 ft (70 cm) long seem to have been divided by internal partitions to get salt cakes of predetermined standard size. Usually, however, the damp crystalline salt was scooped out and packed into porous clay moulds, warmed to 60–70°C to complete the drying. Standard size cakes were aimed at, to facilitate exchange for other goods. At Kimmeridge, on the Isle of Purbeck, the salt moulds were hollow cylinders 3 to 4 in. (70–100 mm) in diameter, with an incision made before firing on either side of the vertical outer wall and also across the bottom. This divided the cylinder into connected halves, a sharp tap along these lines being sufficient to break the vessel into two equal parts and release the dried hardened salt cake intact (Fig. 30).

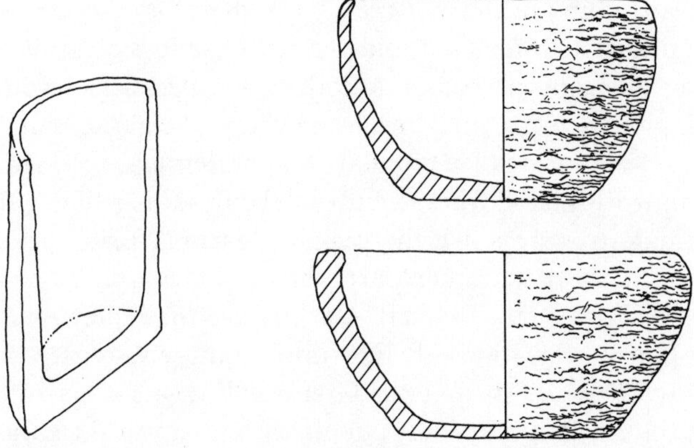

Figure 30. Salt containers from the Isle of Purbeck. After Cunliffe (1974).

Bulk salt production debris, consisting of loose red burnt clay, bar fragments, trays, tray-support debris and container fragments is referred to as *briquetage*. This may accumulate in vast quantities and composes the so-called 'red hills' of the Essex coast, which range in height from 1½ to 6 ft (0.5–2 m) and in area from a few square metres to several hundreds. Much briquetage is also found at Halle on the Saale in Germany, where salt cake moulds of chalice and goblet-like shapes were found, which had been filled with freshly boiled salt and later smashed to extract the hardened salt cake.

Ethnographic evidence also exists for the various methods of salt production by prehistoric people in the present day. Sea water, rock salt and vegetable ashes form the raw material, and the boiled salt cake is always given a definite shape and size, often with the use of special vessels. In tropical countries the salt is dried in the sun, using tubes of matting or cylindrical containers of large leaves, which may then be covered with bast or with a mixture of clay and cow dung.

In Roman times it seems probable that salt extraction was carried out full time by specialists supplying a considerable inland market, rather than by local people producing just enough for families and kinship groups with a small surplus for trade. Classical literature provides many instances of the importance of salt to the Roman world, both as an ingredient in many sacred rites, as a seasoning in cooking and eaten by itself on bread. Pliny, in the *Natural History*, describes the method of extracting salt from lakes and sea water, and states that sea-salt has a sharper flavour than other varieties, a fact which is still exploited today in gourmet cookery. Megaran salt from Greece was especially popular for preserving food in the Roman world, its sharp and bitter flavour adding that 'certain something' to sauces like the popular 'garum', made from the guts of fish 'and the other parts that would normally be considered refuse', soaked in salt. Garum was the liquor obtained from the putrefaction of this unpleasant substance, made originally from a fish that the Greeks called γάρος (garos), but at the time of Pliny the most popular fish used was the scomber, (probably mackerel) obtained from New Carthage. The fish was marketed at nearly 100 sesterces (at least £20) per pint of fish, and the liquid garum was also extremely valuable and widely exported, even to Britain.

The Roman soldier received a salt ration (salarium) as wages which was later paid out in money, hence the present meaning of the word salary. During the Roman occupation of Britain brine pits were opened up inland at Droitwich, Northwich and many other sites. Frere emphasises the ease with which the problems of long distance transport for trade and industry were overcome in Roman Britain. Goods were easily distributed throughout the province via the excellent road network, even large heavy objects such as stone sarcophagi and altars. Carts and wagons were clearly sufficiently developed to carry such heavy cargo, and the road system must have been most efficiently maintained.

Coal makes rare appearances in the ancient world, and seems generally to have been obtained from surface deposits rather than by mining. The earliest finds are from various cremation burials in Welsh Bronze Age cists where it was used, with charcoal, as fuel for the cremation, the coal fragments mixed with coke, burnt clay and burnt and comminuted bone. The pieces are rather small and it has been suggested that it is most unlikely that these are the only burials where coal was used as a fuel, but that it has been missed by the excavators. In Latin the word 'carbo' seems to have been used for both charcoal and coal, and which of the two is meant is not always clear from the context. The Romans, although intensely practical, lacked the scientific spirit of enquiry, and although coal had relatively widespread use in Roman Britain and was locally available, they failed to realise its great economic and industrial potential. Sufficient fuel such as timber, was readily available in the south, and the coal outcrops of the west and north of the country were certainly exploited, but not mined. Most of the Romano-British finds of coal occur near outcrops, and Webster draws a map to show just how strong the correlation is. This implies that large-scale long-distance transport of coal was not practised in Roman Britain, although the extensive use of coal by the Wall garrisons and nearby military depots probably indicates some central organisation for its digging and distribution which was probably in operation at least by the middle of the 2nd century. The first Roman occurrence is at Heronnbridge (near Chester), dated to AD 90–130. Coal also appears at some of the forts on the Antonine wall but large quantities have been found on the forts associated with Hadrian's wall, including about one ton in the guard chamber of the east gate at Housesteads. This last deposit was found in a chamber which seems to have been converted into a coal store in about the early 4th century. Coal seems to have been supplied officially to forts, and elsewhere it was used for firing hypocausts (the Roman underfloor central heating system), and in some smithing furnaces. Some private villas were also supplied, especially those in Gloucestershire, Somerset and Wiltshire where coal could be obtained from the nearby Somerset outcrops. These same sources probably produced the coal used on the altar of the goddess Sulis Minerva at Bath, which was recorded as a curiosity by Solinus in the 3rd century, 'In Britain are hot springs furnished luxuriously for human use. Over these springs Minerva presides and in her temple the perpetual fire never whitens into ash but as the flame fades turns into rocky balls' (Solinus, *Collectanea rerum memorabilium*). Bath was undoubtedly one of the chief religious centres of Roman Britain at this time. Solinus is clearly referring to coal, and the terms which he uses convey the feeling that it was still something of a natural curiosity, and at the time of writing far from being a common form of fuel.

CHAPTER 7

Ritual, religion and magic

'So far, everything that has given colour to existence lacks a history'
(Nietzsche, 1882)

It is unfortunate that in the present day the study of the manifestations of so-called 'ritual' behaviour is one of the most hazardous (and currently unfashionable) branches of archaeology due to its empirical nature. The practitioners of the 'New' archaeology have endeavoured to cram archaeology into what they believe to be an empirical scientific framework, but this has often resulted in the wholesale borrowing of fashionable techniques from other disciplines and forcing archaeological data into them, whether or not they are suitable, in a desperate search for 'quantification'. The extremes of the 'New 'archaeology are, however, only the most obvious demonstrations of an underlying basic trend, which emphasises the empirical at the expense of the hypothetical. Ritual behaviour of any kind falls, unfortunately, into the latter category, and there seems to be a general feeling that to interpret any feature as possibly 'of ritual significance' is academically indecent, an admission of defeat on the part of the excavator who has been unable to find any more concrete reason for its existence.

Early societies obviously held views about the supernatural world very different from those which we hold today. In the modern world religion is frequently regarded as an optional extra or a comfort in times of trouble, any form of ritual behaviour being taken as a manifestation of this. If one's life is at the whim of Nature, and Nature is controlled by the Gods, more respect must be paid to them and the correct forms and customs observed, even if their origin has long since been divorced from their current meaning. It is impossible for us, in our hygienic mental climate, to understand or sympathise with such views, and even the rather attractive pantheons of the Classical world are regarded with suspicion on the grounds that their members seem too human to be divine. Our own particular god, if we believe in one, tends to be seen as a rather remote semi-abstract concept, whose rewards for virtue or punishments for vice are conveniently deferred until after death. In early societies the supernatural was part of the very fabric of life, the gods always watching, waiting and acting. This then is the rich basis for mythology, and it is a pity that any fragmentary extract of early religious/ritual beliefs has to be interpreted in the light of the climate of present thinking. This problem was discussed by Jaquetta Hawkes with reference to the palaeo-astronomical work carried out at Stonehenge. She said, 'The obvious view is whether, because this last view of Stonehenge belongs to a scientific age supposedly concerned with objective truth it must approximate more nearly to what Stonehenge meant to its builders, or whether it might be just as much affected by contemporary interests and modes of thought as the views of the former romantics and classicists'.

The general cynicism about ritual behaviour is currently reflected particularly clearly in the study of prehistoric stone monuments, especially henges. On one side are the archaeologists who have attempted sensible and systematic studies of the megalith-builders' construction techniques and astronomy, and on the other the parapsychologists who have postulated flying saucers and extra-terrestrial influences. Unfortunately the latter school of thought is the one which has by far the more popular appeal, as can be shown by an examination of any current 'best seller' list, which is sure to include at least one book produced by the 'was-God-an-astronaut' school. Henge monuments and other megalithic constructions have caught the public fancy for two reasons: first because they are so large, obvious and impossible to miss; and secondly because they serve no apparent purpose and are thus ripe for specula-

Figure 31.

tion as to how they were constructed, and why. The first question has been successfully answered, and it has already been demonstrated (p. 90) that the secret of moving large stones lies in well-motixated and organised gangs of workmen, rather than in the 'spacemen' whose presence is seemingly indispensable to the more credulous.

In these days of automation it has become difficult to visualise such huge weights as having been moved by human labour alone, and this has led to the accumulation of a body of legend that the stones were able to move themselves. John Coles, in a recent book concerned with experimental archaeology illustrates this theory, and quotes a charming description of some South American megalithic stones found between the quarry and their destination, and called *piedras cansadas* ('tired stones'). It is, however, clear from a study of what literature survives concerning the *modus operandi* of ancient stone constructions that ritual and spells probably played an important part in the process at the time, both for the encouragement and reward of the workers and to provide an alternative 'reason why' to the basic desire to make something spectacular and impressive, to act as a symbol of power to the glory of a ruler, his people, or his gods.

Myths and legends connected with field monuments (especially henges) are legion and have become inextricably confused with their archaeology. Hardly a circle of standing stones exists without a ghostly background of lithified, dancing giants or witches, nor a collection of burial tumuli without its legends. The faintly superstitious feeling, produced by a tumulus, the awareness of what had once been there, the 'pricking of the thumbs', was evoked to perfection by J. R. R. Tolkien when he created the sinister Barrow-wights, encountered in unpleasant circumstances by Frodo on a foggy day on the Barrow-Downs.

From the realms of the supernatural we move to the more prosaic paths of megalithic engineering, a field in which much progress has been made in recent years principally owing to the efforts of Professor Alexander Thom. His findings not only reveal that henges were built to standard plans using standard units of measurement (the so-called 'megalithic yard') but also that megalithic man appears to have been observing the moon and recording his findings with great accuracy. Thom asserts that the henge-builders had achieved a knowledge of the motions of the moon which was not to be improved on for over three thousand years. Aspects of his work have been criticised by mathematicians and astronomers, but in the main his theories have won reluctant but widespread support, and in 1972 the editor of *Antiquity* commented that '. . . no reasonable archaeologist can do other than give Thom's work the most serious consideration'. There will always be those who remain unconvinced, and while accepting that Stonehenge was intended primarily as a sanctuary, view the 'celestial observatory' theory as a manifestation of the scientific wishful thinking so characteristically a product of our time. Perhaps they are right.

Whether or not we consider that henges are of 'scientific' importance their 'ritual' significance cannot be denied. 'Ritual' buildings, i.e. buildings used primarily for magical or religious ceremonies, have existed since Palaeolithic times, our cathedrals today performing essentially the same function as painted caves did for a technologically less sophisticated society. The desire and ability to build large-scale co-operative monuments has been taken as one of the parameters for defining civilisation. Sometimes, however, large quantities of stone seem to have been moved for no apparent purpose whatsoever, or at least no purpose which is obvious to us today. The Olmec culture of Mesoamerica, flourishing between 1200 and 600 BC, is particularly famous for its weird but original art style, exemplified in the carving of huge basalt heads, up to 8 ft (2.4 m) high, often wearing helmets and with characteristically puffy lips. Strange, sexless human figurines with the same loose-lipped malevolence are also found, sometimes carved to resemble a snarling jaguar. At the Olmec ceremonial centre of La Venta four of the massive heads were found, together with caches of figurines, jade axes and rectangular pits filled with layers of serpentine blocks, in one case amounting to a total of 12 000 tons. Some of the axes were beautifully carved in dark green jade, many showing again the typical Olmec face. All this basalt, serpentine and jade must have been brought to the site from hundreds of miles away, and it seems to have served no practical purpose. At least 5000 tons of serpentine and even more basalt was brought between 100 and 350 miles (160–560 km) by water, an undertaking implying a great deal of pressure and control by a central heirarchy, probably a small priestly caste ruling over a large and unwieldy mass of peasants. However, some authorities think that a special merchant class existed, who traded Olmec goods back from the ceremonial centres up into the highland areas where the stone sources lay. The centres where the rulers lived seem to have been primarily religious, being undefended and with no indications of any warlike activity. Here, surely, is an example of large-scale stone transport for purely ritual or ceremonial purposes.

The recurring importance of jade is especially interesting, and has been discussed above. Jade as a substance was frequently associated with burial rituals, often being thought to

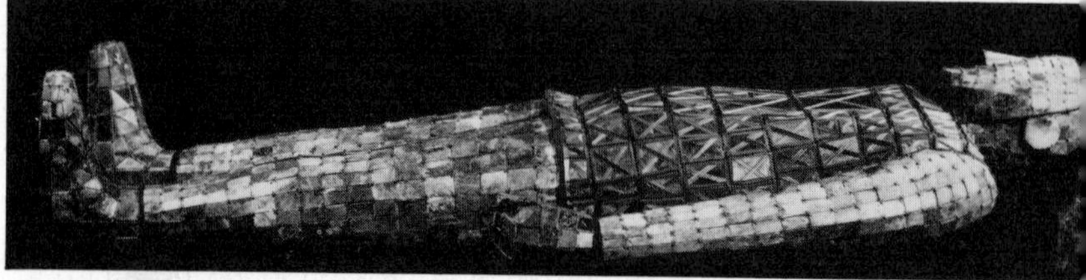

Figure 32. Jade funeral suite of Princess Tou Wan, late 2nd century BC, Hopei, China. Reproduced by kind permission of Times Newspapers Ltd and Robert Harding Associates.

have magical powers. Amulets made of it were much favoured in the Middle Ages, as they were believed to protect their wearers from kidney diseases, the name of the substance being derived from the Spanish *hijada* (kidney). In China Taoist lore included a belief that jade would prevent the decay of a corpse, and burials are often found where small pieces of jade have been placed to seal the nine orifices of the body, and a cicada of jade laid on the tongue. The most impressive jade finds of this kind are undoubtedly the funeral suits of Prince Liu Sheng and his wife Princess Tou Wan (Fig. 32), who lived during the late 2nd century BC. The suits, which completely covered the bodies, were elaborate developments of the basic preservation idea. That of the princess was made of 2160 individual tablets of jade, varying in size from $\frac{5}{8} \times \frac{3}{8}$ in. (1.5 × 1 cm) to $2\frac{1}{8} \times 1\frac{3}{8}$ in (5.4 × 3.5 cm) and in thickness from $\frac{1}{8}$ to $\frac{3}{16}$ in. (2–3.5 mm). The component units of the suit (gloves, arms, legs, shoes, head, back and front of torso) were made separately, and attached by a stitching of gold wires passed through holes at the corners of the tablets, except across the chest where the tablets were attached by tapes to a heavy cloth lining. It seems that the jade was probably imported from Sinkiang, hundreds of miles to the west of the burial site at Man-Ch'enj in Hopei province. The head of the body lay on a pillow of gilded bronze, inlaid with jade, and the burial was accompanied by very rich grave goods, including a series of 6 jade rings (*pi*) of a form which first appears in the Chinese Neolithic several thousand years earlier. It seems to have a symbolic meaning associated with burial. Third century BC ritual texts describe the *pi* as a symbol of the sky appropriate for the emperors' use when performing a sacrifice to heaven (Fig. 33). *Pi* are placed in burials at either side of the head, and on each knee. Simpler penannular rings of white jade (nephrite) and the more popular green variety are found even earlier than the *pi*, and also seem to have had some form of symbolic meaning. Similar ones were made in the Baikal region of Siberia, one of the source areas for Chinese jade, the simpler rings pre-dating the elaborately engraved *pi*. The nephrite was worked by a lengthy treatment using a powdered abrasive, a technique also used in the Balkans and Urals.

This belief in the preservative power of a particular type of stone is far from unique in folklore. Red ochre is often found in association with burials, probably used as a life-symbol because of its blood-red colour. In one of the Grimaldi caves on the south coast of France a cache of some 8000 small shells was found mixed with red ochre in a burial, and the pigment was also used for painting figurines and decorating skeletons in the early Neolithic sites of Haçilar and Çatal Hüyük. It was found staining the bones of the famous Upper Palaeolithic 'Red lady' of Paviland cave, South Wales, actually the skeleton of a young

Figure 33. Carved jade discs, *pi*, of the type used by the Chinese emperor when performing sacrifices to heaven.

man, probably about twenty-five years old, who had been ceremonially buried in the extended position under a covering of red ochre, apparently in deliberate association with a mammoth skull. This type of situation is not confined to Europe, and some of the pre-Classical cultures of the Valley of Mexico also used red, haematite-derived, pigments to cover the dead. The bodies were placed either in shallow pits or in formal tombs floored with clean beach sand and covered with stone slabs. Ochre, of course, was also used extensively as a cosmetic and as a painting medium. Haematite also has medico-religious uses and was thought by the Romans to be good for bloodshot eyes, bladder trouble and, when mixed with human milk, for filling cavities left by sores and 'also suitable for reducing protruding eyes' (Pliny, *Natural History*, 36.147).

Jet has a related folklore: 'the kindling of jet drives off snakes and relieves suffocation of the uterus. Its fumes detect attempts to simulate a disabling illness or a state of virginity' (Pliny, op. cit. 36.138). This is a comic, but sincere, example of the close links between ritual, magic and medicine which existed in the ancient world.

Certain types of minerals, stones and fossils, seem repeatedly to turn up in association with early cultural remains, and it is sometimes difficult to see whether they were being kept as charms, amulets, the means to prevent accidents or disease or the means to cure them. Often, no doubt, they were valued for all these purposes, as in the cases already quoted. Caches of charms and amulets abound, and there is a fine example from an otherwise empty burial cist in a cairn at Aberdeen. Over 50 natural stones and a dozen artifacts were found, including two echinoids (*Galenites* or *Conulus*) from the Peterhead Drift or the Chalk of eastern England, stones of chalcedony and agate, amber, flint and quartz, stones with striking natural marking (such as a dark red jasper with a white stratum running through it), and stones of especially attractive appearance (such as a blue silicified mudstone). The collection includes some flint implements, a perforated ornament and an imitation sardonyx intaglio of moulded glass. Many of the natural stones were abraded and the finder suggests that the collection either represents a hiding place for valuables, the cairn being used to give it an aura of sanctity, or that the deposition of the material was made as an offering to the spirits of the cairn.

Prehistoric arrowheads and other flints, particularly the barbed and tanged forms common in Upper Palaeolithic and Bronze Age times have a folklore all of their own, and sickness in cattle has been attributed by country people to these objects which they believed to have been 'elf bolts' shot at the animals by fairies. When the arrowheads were collected they were labelled 'elf shot' well into the 19th century, and preserved for medicinal use since the water in which they have been boiled was believed to be beneficial to diseased cattle, for some seemingly illogical reason.

The desire to collect fossils seems to have been present even in the most primitive societies, although certain types appear to have attracted more notice than others, probably because they were either fairly common or of especially striking appearance. Presumably this tendency is a result of the belief that such fossils were 'lucky', or else that they were simply being collected as curios. Figure 34 shows some splendid examples of ammonites, which hold a unique place in the folklore of fossils because of their resemblance to a coiled snake. It is rather difficult to distinguish between snake and ammonite in art and legend, but we know that the former, at any rate, holds a special place in the folklore of primitive peoples. Odd ammonites turn up as charms and the fossils were thought to be a protection against serpents, and cure for baldness, impotence and barrenness. In India a draught of water in which one of the sacred ammonites has been steeped is supposed to wash away any sin and secure temporal welfare, a form of the Vishnu cult which has been traced on literary evidence back to the 5th century BC. The Liassic rocks of north Yorkshire are rich in ammonites, which were described by Camden in 1586 as the 'Whitby snakestones', since the fossils were thought once to have been living serpents until St Hilda destroyed them, and they were without heads as the result of St Cuthbert's curse. Some of the Whitby dealers obviously felt that it was inconvenient to have headless snakes and carved some fresh ones, of which splendid examples are shown in Figure 34, from the collections of the Natural History Museum, London.

The pointed guard of the belemnite occurs commonly in Jurassic and Cretaceous rocks, and specimens have been described as 'Devils Fingers', 'St Peter's Fingers', or taken to be thunderbolts. A public house near Wimbourne in Dorset rejoices in the unusual, and possibly unique, name of 'St Peter's Fingers', probably named after finds of belemnites

Figure 34. A selection of ammonites with snake heads added. Modified specimens of *Hildoceras* sp. and *Dactylioceras* sp. Reproduced by kind permission of the Trustees of the British Museum, Natural History.

made from local outcrops of Cretaceous rocks. A smoothed belemnite was found in a Bronze Age barrow at Langton Wold, in Yorkshire, and there is a mass of folklore describing the fossils as thunderstones or thunderbolts.

Echinoids are often found in the south of England as flint casts derived from the Chalk, and are another series of fossils which have stimulated a large folklore. The common names for them are 'shepherds' crowns', 'shepherds' purses' or 'fairy loaves', and the writer has found that the workers in the Hampshire gravel pits usually regard them as lucky, rows of them being kept to adorn the windows of excavating machinery. Oakley records the common practice of placing echinoids on dairy shelves to keep the milk from going sour, a practice clearly associated with the vague idea that these fossils like belemnites are thunderbolts, and lightning is well known never to strike twice in the same place! At a ceremonial burial of early Bronze Age date in a barrow on the Dunstable Downs nearly 100 'shepherds' crowns', mainly *Micraster* sp., were arranged to encircle the bodies of a woman and child although the excavator's reconstruction reproduced in Figure 35 shows far more than a little wishful thinking. Another superstition seems to be that if one finds an echinoid one should spit on it and throw it over the left shoulder for luck, much in the same way that a pinch of salt is tossed to blind the devil who usually stands there. Blinkenberg describes the find of a flint *Conulus* from an Iron Age grave in Denmark, which had been mounted in bronze and appeared to be used as an amulet. A whole tradition has also grown up about the supposed magical powers of the echinoid, especially as an antidote for poison. In Medieval times wine in which sharks' teeth had been steeped was also regarded as an antidote to poison and snake bites, and they were also considered to be protection against the evil eye. Substances are chosen as amulets either for their shape or for some other distinctive property, such as colour. Blue has always been a favourite colour, and was used for talismans as far back as predynastic times in Egypt, and is still in use today. In the Middle East turquoise, obtained from mines in Iran and Afghanistan, is still worn by poor people as a charm. Until

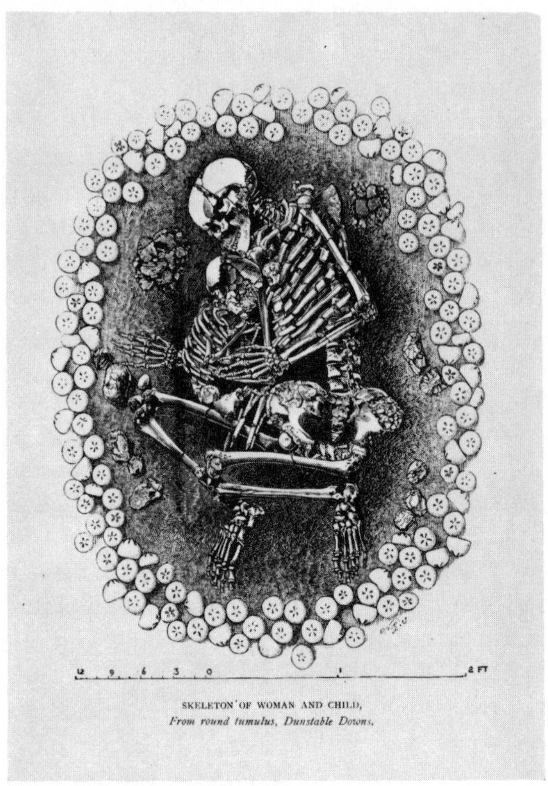

Figure 35. A reconstruction drawing made by Worthington Smith (1894) of a burial of a woman and child surrounded by echinoids of the species *Ananchytes ovatus* and *Micraster cor-anguinium*. Smith records at least 220 of these together with a single pebble of white quartz and various animal bones, but this symmetrical reconstruction is fanciful.

recently the stone was usually set in droplets, worn by women across the foreheads, but lucky turquoise beads even adorned donkeys, and carts. This is but one minor example of the continuing tradition of stone-using and stone-working, both in historic and in prehistoric times. Stone was the first resource to be exploited and the basis for early technology. More artefacts, from houses to handaxes, are made of stone than of any other substance, and it can surely be said, as a paraphrase of Oakley's famous aphorism, that 'rocks maketh man'.

References

FURTHER READING

Forbes, R. J. 1964. *Studies in ancient technology*, 7 vols. Leiden: E. J. Brill.

Herodotus. *The Histories.*

Hodges, H. W. M. 1964. *Artefacts: an introduction to early materials and technology*, London: John Baker.

Levey, M. 1959. *Chemistry and chemical technology in ancient Mesopotamia.* Amsterdam/London/NewYork: Elsevier.

Lucas, A. 1948. *Ancient Egyptian materials and industries*, 3rd rev. edn. London: Edward Arnold.

Lucretius. *De Rerum Natura.*

Oakley, K. P. 1965. Folklore of fossils, Part 1. *Antiquity* XXXIX, 9–17.

Oakley, K. P. 1965. Folklore of fossils, Part 2. *Antiquity* XXXIX, 117–26.

Oakley, K. P. 1975. *Decorative and symbolic uses of vertebrate fossils.* London: Oxford University Press.

Pliny the Elder. *Natural History.*

Rochlin, G. I. 1974. *Scientific technology and social change.* San Francisco: W. H. Freeman.

Singer, C., E. J. Holmyard and A. R. Hall 1954. *A history of technology.* London: Oxford University Press.

Strabo. *The Geography.*

Theophrastus. *History of stones.*

SELECTED BIBLIOGRAPHIES

Chapter 1

Bromehead, C. N. 1945. Geology in embryo. *Proceedings of the Geologists Association*, **56,** 89–134.

Childe, V. G. 1957. *The dawn of European civilization.* London. Routledge and Kegan Paul.

Holmes, A. 1944. *Principles of physical geology.* London: Nelson.

Piggott, S. 1965. *Ancient Europe.* Edinburgh: Edinburgh University Press.

Read, H. H. 1971. *Rutley's elements of mineralogy*, 26th edn. London: George Allen & Unwin/Thomas Murby.

Sparks, B. W. 1960. *Geomorphology.* London: Longman.

Wallis, F. S. 1949. Rocks and the archaeologist. *Trans. Bristol and Glos. Arch. Soc.* LXXXIX, 155–73.

Woods, H. 1963. *Palaeontology: invertebrate*, 8th edn. Cambridge: Cambridge University Press.

Chapter 2

Boon, G. C. 1967. Micaceous sigillata from Lezoux at Silchester, Caerleon and other sites. *Antiq. J.* **47,** 27–43.

Bushnell, G. H. S. 1956. *Peru.* London: Thames and Hudson.

Cann, J. R. and C. Renfrew 1964. The characterisation of obsidian and its application to the Mediterranean region. *Proc. prehist. soc.* **30,** 111–34.

Coles, J., B. Orme, A. C. Bishop and A. R. Wooley 1974. A jade axe from the Somerset levels. *Antiquity* XLVIII, 216–20.

Cummins, W. A. 1974. The Neolithic stone axe trade in Britain. *Antiquity,* XLVIII, 201–6.

Hodder, I. 1973. Regression analysis of some trade and marketing patterns. *World Archaeology* **6** (2), 172–90.

Leakey, L. S. B. 1965. *Olduvai Gorge, 1951–1961, Vol. 1. Preliminary report on the geology and fauna.* Cambridge: Cambridge University Press.

Peacock, D. P. S. 1967. The heavy mineral analysis of pottery: a preliminary report. *Archaeometry* **10,** 97–101.

Renfrew, A. C., J. E. Dixon and J. R. Cann 1966. Obsidian and early cultural contact in the Near East. *Proc. prehist. soc.* **32,** 30–74.

Renfrew, A. C., J. E. Dixon and J. R. Cann 1968. Further analysis of Near Eastern obsidian. *Proc. prehist. soc.* **34,** 319–31.

Sieveking, G., P. Bush, J. Ferguson, P. T. Craddock, M. J. Hughes and M. R. Cowell 1972. Prehistoric flint mines and their identification as sources of raw material. *Archaeometry* **14,** 151–77.

Smith, W. C. 1963. Jade axes from sites in the British Isles. *Proc. prehist. soc.* **29,** 133–72.

Vaillant, G. C. 1944. *The Aztecs of Mexico.* New York: Doubleday.

Watson, W. 1973. *The genius of China: catalogue to the Chinese exhibition.* London: Times Newspapers Ltd.

Washburn, S. L. 1974. Tools and human evolution. In *Scientific technology and social change,* G. I. Rochlin (ed.). San Francisco: W. H. Freeman.

Chapter 3

Augusti, S. 1957. La technique de la Peinture Pompeienne. *Edizioni Technique* (Napoli).

Davey, N. 1961. *A history of building materials.* London: Phoenix.

Frere, S. S. 1967. *Britannia.* London: Routledge and Kegan Paul.

Vitruvius. *De Architectura.*

Chapter 4

Atkinson, R. J. C. 1960. *Stonehenge.* London: Penguin Books.

Edwards, I. E. S. 1947. *The Pyramids of Egypt.* London: Penguin Books.

Hawkes, J. 1968. *Dawn of the Gods.* London: Chatto and Windus.

Jope, E. M. 1964. The Saxon building – stone industry in southern and midland England. *Medieval Archaeology* **8,** 91–118.

Powell, T. G. E. 1969. *Megalithic enquiries.* Liverpool: Liverpool University Press.

Renfrew, A. C. 1973. *Before civilization.* London: Methuen.

Stone, E. H. 1924. *The stones of Stonehenge.* London: Scott.

Taylor, H. M. 1965. *Anglo-Saxon architecture*, 2 vols. Cambridge: Cambridge University Press.

Chapter 5

Beck, C., E. Wilbur, S. Meret, M. Kossova and K. Kermani 1965. The infrared spectra of amber and the identification of Baltic amber. *Archaeometry* **8,** 96–110.

Bennett, C. M. 1967. A cosmetic palette from Umm-el-Biyara. *Antiquity* XLI, 197–201.

Boardman, J. 1970. *Greek gems and finger rings*. London: Thames and Hudson.

Bordes, F. 1968. *The Old Stone Age*. London: Weidenfeld and Nicolson.

Cunliffe, B. W. 1974. *Iron age communities in Britain*. London: Routledge and Kegan Paul.

Evans, J. 1922. *Magical jewels of the Middle Ages and the Renaissance, particularly in England*. Oxford: Milford.

King, C. W. 1860. *Antique gems*. London: John Murray.

Mellaart, J. 1965. *Earliest civilizations of the Near East*. London: Thames and Hudson.

Petrie, W. M. F. 1909. *The arts and crafts of ancient Egypt*. Edinburgh and London: Nelson.

Rottlander, R. C. A. 1970. On the formation of amber from *pinus* resin. *Archaeometry* **12,** (1), 35–51.

Weidmann, A. 1892. Varieties of ancient kohl in *Medum* Petrie, W. F. M. London: Brit. School of Arch. in Egypt.

Williamson, G. C. 1932. *The book of amber*. London: Benn.

Chapter 6

Collingwood, R. G. 1937. *An economic survey of Ancient Rome*. Baltimore: John Hopkins Press.

Gadd, C. J. and R. C. Thompson 1941. A middle Babylonian chemical text. *Iraq* **III,** 87–8.

Needham, J. 1959. *Science and civilization in China*. Cambridge: Cambridge University Press.

North, F. J. 1940. A geologist among the cairns. *Antiquity* **14,** 377–94.

Rawlinson, H. C. 1861. *A selection from the historical inscriptions of Chaldaea, Assyria and Babylonia*. London: British Museum.

Reed, R. 1972. *Ancient skins, parchments and leathers*. London: Seminar Press.

Reisner, G. A. 1905. *The Hearst medical papyrus*. Hearst Egyptian expedition Vol. 1. Leipzig.

Riehm, K. 1961. Prehistoric salt-boiling. *Antiquity* **35,** 181–91.

Strassmaier, J. N. 1889. *Inschriften von Nebuchodonosor, Konig von Babylon 604–561 v. Chr.* Babylonische Texte. Leipzig.

Thompson, R. C. 1908. Assyrian prescriptions for diseases of the head. Reprint *Am. Journal of Semitic Lang. and Lit.* **24.** Chicago.

Thompson, R. C. 1923. Assyrian medical texts from the originals in the British Museum, London. *Am. Journal of Semitic Lang. and Lit.* XXIV(4) Chicago.

Webster, G. 1955. A note on the use of coal in Roman Britain. *Antiq. J.* **35,** 199–217.

Chapter 7

Coles, J. 1973. *Archaeology by experiment.* London: Hutchinson.

Koenigswald, G. H. R. 1956. *Meeting prehistoric man.* London: Thames and Hudson.

Hawkes, J. 1967. God in the machine. *Antiquity* **41,** 174–80.

Smith, W. G. 1894. *Man, the primeval savage.* London. Edward Stanford.

Thom, A. 1967. *Megalithic sites in Britain.* Oxford: Clarendon Press.

Whitehouse, F. W. 1958. The Australian Aboriginal as a collector of fossils. *Queensland Naturalist* **13,** 100–2.

Index